HART CRANE'S
THE BRIDGE

THE

Studies in the Humanities No. 20   *Literature*

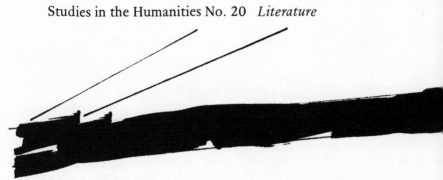

ART CRANE'S
BRIDGE

Description of Its Life

ichard P. Sugg

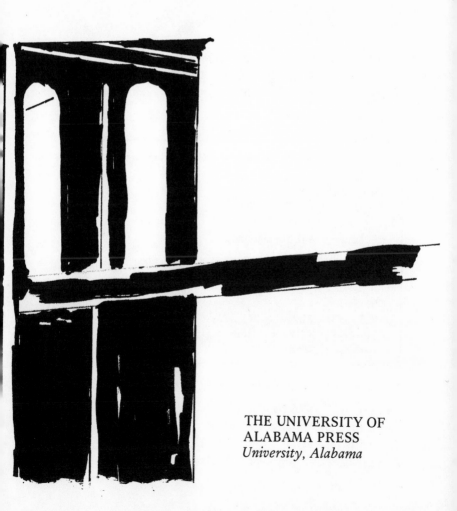

THE UNIVERSITY OF
ALABAMA PRESS
University, Alabama

Library of Congress Cataloging in Publication Data

Sugg, Richard P
    Hart Crane's *The Bridge*.

    (Studies in the humanities)
    Bibliography: p. 124
    Includes index.
    1. Crane, Hart, 1899-1932. The bridge. I. Title.
II. Series.
PS3505.R272B738   811',5'2   76-15241
ISBN 0-8173-7104-4 (Cloth)
ISBN 0-8173-7105-2 (Paper)

CONTENTS

ACKNOWLEDGMENTS

I would like to thank all those who in various ways contributed to the making of this book. It was my great good fortune to meet William R. Robinson during that crucial period when I first contemplated writing about Hart Crane's THE BRIDGE; his rare combination of a radically creative intelligence and a passionate commitment to the necessity of individual freedom and self-discovery made him the ideal mentor. During the ensuing eight years, intellectual and emotional contributions were made by many others, including Professors John B. Pickard and Ants Oras, Frances Fevrier, Francis M. and Valerie Burke, Dale and Penny Myers, Robert Nadeau, Richard Messer, Sarah Lynch DeMellier, and Mrs. Carolyn Sherman. I would like to thank also Arkansas State University and the University of Kentucky for grants which helped make this book possible.

RICHARD P. SUGG

To my Mother

PART I
Hart Crane's Dream of Act

CHAPTER ONE

Hart Crane's Aesthetics

Hart Crane's poetry, and especially *The Bridge*, has been and will continue to be misunderstood as long as the poet's belief in and commitment to the life of the imagination remains unclear. His "dream of act," supported by his confidence in the imagination's power to create worlds, self-sustaining and evocative of new states of consciousness, finds its most significant articulation and realization in *The Bridge*. It is encouraging that both the popularity and critical appreciation of Crane's greatest poem have increased in recent years. For whatever reasons, the contemporary audience is more appreciative of his avowed attempt to discover "under new forms certain spiritual illuminations, shining with a morality essentialized from experience directly, and not from previous precepts or preconceptions."[1] It has not always been so. The critical history of *The Bridge*, reflecting the evolution of twentieth century thought and literary criticism, testifies to the profundity and insight of the poem. For the critics have learned from as well as about the poem, and its reputation has grown as they found their knowledge confirmed in other areas of human endeavor. So it should be. Certain great poetry, Eliot reminds us, must create its own audience, or wait upon their education. *The Bridge* deserves a closer study than it has previously been given, one that will bear witness to the poem's powers—not only to endure but to educate.

The early and adverse response to *The Bridge* was motivated, at least in part, from certain critics' belief that poetry should speak to the moral and political problems of the world, if not in fact solve them. Allen Tate and Yvor Winters, whom Crane counted among his friends and peers, agreed that the poem failed of its epical ambitions.[2] They attacked Crane's choice of the Brooklyn Bridge as an attempt "to put greater pressure of meaning upon a trivial symbol than it would bear,"[3] and objected to the absence of the kind of unity and coherence which they expected from the traditional, "cultural" epic. Tate cogently stated the case against Crane's epic of the lyrical imagination: "His pantheism is necessarily a philosophy of sensation without point of view. An epic is a judgment of human action, an implied evaluation of a civilization, a way of life."[4] R. P. Blackmur echoed and enlarged on Tate's criticism when in 1935, declaring that *The Waste Land*, *The Cantos*, and *The Bridge* were the most ambitious poems of his time, he pronounced all three failures "in composition, in independent objective existence, and in intelligibility of language."[5] Crane responded to these objections by asserting that it is not poetry's main purpose to serve the aims of philosophy:

> Taggard, like Winters, isn't looking for poetry anymore. Like Munson, they are both in pursuit of some cure-all. Poetry as poetry (and I don't mean merely decorative verse) isn't worth a second reading anymore. Therefore—away with Kubla Khan, out with Marlowe, and to hell with Keats! It's a pity, I think. So many true things have a way of coming out all the better without the strain to sum up the universe in one impressive little pellet. I

admit that I don't answer the requirements. My vision of poetry is too personal to "answer the call."[6]

In the last two decades critics have been more appreciative of Crane's assumptions about poetry, offering readings of *The Bridge* as "a romantic lyric given epic implications"[7] in which American history becomes "an enlarged or collective version of the romantic poet's biography,"[8] or seeing in the poem "the gradual permeation of an entire culture by the power of poetic vision."[9] Even so, these later theories about *The Bridge* seem to assign the poem a principle of order based on its representation of something other than the poetic act: Dembo sees the formal principle as one in which for the poet "resurrection always follows suffering and death,"[10] and Lewis argues that the poem's form is a rhythm of "vision briefly enjoyed, vision lost, vision recovered"[11] by the poet. Implicit in both these arguments is that *The Bridge* is about the poet's relationship with the world; my own belief is that *The Bridge* is about the poetic act rather than the action of the poet as a person in the world, about the life of the imagination trying to realize its "dream of act" by giving form, and thereby meaning, to itself.

Thus the "continuous and eloquent span"[12] of *The Bridge* must be described within the context of Crane's poetic beliefs and practices, for its very structure depends upon the movement of the imagination, the hero of this "epic of the modern consciousness,"[13] towards the creation of a poem, the fulfillment of its dream of act. And that movement proceeds along lines most explicit in Crane's own comments on his poetry. He scornfully warned the critic Gorham Munson against seeking "exact factual data (a graphic map of eternity?), ethical morality or moral classifications, etc.":

you arbitrarily propose a goal for me which I have no idea of nor interest in following. Either you find my work poetic or not, but

if you propose for it such ends as *poetry organically escapes,* it
seems to me, as Allen (Tate) said, that you as a critic of literature
are working into a confusion of categories.[14] [italics mine]

Not only is *The Bridge* constructed according to Crane's
theory of organic poetry, and hence to some extent explicable
in terms of his poetics; but also, *The Bridge* is a poem about
the creation of a poem, one that can embody the truth of the
fictional poet's imagination in "one arc synoptic" ("Atlantis"). The poem, then, not only results from a process of
organic creation, it also continually celebrates and re-enacts
that process as its proper subject. Thus to propose a goal for,
or a critical appreciation of, *The Bridge* which is based on
categories or intentions not inherent in Crane's poetic purposes is to run that risk of a confusion of categories. In the
American tradition of Emerson and Whitman, Crane was not
concerned with society except insofar as it proceeded from
the life of the individual, which for the poet means the life of
the individual's imagination. Such poetry "teaches" society
by evincing that life. As Crane's contemporary Wallace
Stevens noted, "The subject-matter of poetry is not that
'collection of solid, static objects extended in space' but the
life that is lived in the scene that it composes; and so reality
is not that eternal scene but the life that is lived in it."[15]
Neither Crane nor *The Bridge* intend any more (nor any less)
than is implicit in "giving form to the living stuff of the
imagination."[16]

There are three major aspects of Crane's poetic theory
which bear on the nature and direction of *The Bridge*: the
process by which a poem is created, the kind of poem resulting from this process, and the function of the poem in relation
to the reader. The creative process is an organic one in which
the poet submits to experience, assimilates and unifies it,
then represents to the world the evidence of this unifying of
experience within a poem.

The actual fleshing of a concept is so complex and difficult, however, as to be quite beyond the immediate avail of will or intellect. A fusion with other factors not so easily named is the condition of fulfillment. It is all right to call this "possession," if you will, only it should not be insisted that its operation denies the simultaneous function of a strong critical faculty. It is simply a stronger focus that can be arbitrarily willed into operation by the ordinarily-employed perceptions.[17]

The organic metaphor for the creative process, "the fleshing of a concept," suggests the supra-rational origin of the poem that will carry what Crane called "the very blood and bone of me."[18]

For Crane, as for Stevens, a poem is not about external reality, but about the imagination's attempts to assimilate and unify external reality in its own life. Thus a poem is a record of the imagination's life, and a narrative poem like The Bridge is a record of one man's growth toward unity through history and place, when history and place are considered not only ultimately inseparable from but also originating in his own varying states of consciousness. The poet redeems the possibilities of the future by living through and integrating the past and present. But he doesn't redeem the future by romantically asserting some brand of Pollyanna optimism, or by proving that machines aren't all bad, or anything of that sort. He redeems it by demonstrating through his own example that the human imagination has a life that can assimilate, unify and grow beyond any experience of time or place, that the human imagination is itself a bridge uniting past and present and leading to the future:

It is my hope to go *through* the combined materials of the poem, using our "real" world somewhat as a springboard, and to give the poem *as a whole* an orbit or predetermined direction of its own. . . . Its evocation will not be toward decoration or amusement, but rather toward a state of consciousness, an "innocence"

(Blake) or absolute beauty. In this condition there may be discoverable under new forms certain spiritual illuminations, shining with a morality essentialized from experience directly, and not from previous precepts or preconceptions. It is as though a poem gave the reader as he left it a single, new *word*, never before spoken and impossible to actually enunciate, but self-evident as an active principle in the reader's consciousness henceforward.[19]

The goal of the process is simultaneously moral and aesthetic, evincing what Nietzsche called "the trans-valuation of values" by which the aesthetic precedes the moral and Beauty really does become Truth. Crane said that goal was the only "absolute" to which he subscribed, this unitive state of consciousness characterized by "'innocence' (Blake) or absolute beauty." What Crane's poetry teaches, then, is how to live life according to the laws of the imagination. Stevens posited this as the major concern of modern poetry in declaring that the poet's function "is to make his imagination theirs (the readers') and that he fulfills himself only as he sees his imagination become the light in the minds of others.[20] The art for which Crane strives, then, is truly organic and living, born of a vital process and committed to engendering further life. Its goal is not a cessation of speech, but an evocation of the "single, new *word*" that can "germinate new forms of spiritual articulations." Crane described both the process and its goal by quoting Blake: "I give you the end of a golden string:/ Only wind it into a ball—/ It will lead you in at Heaven's gate,/ Built in Jerusalem's wall."[21]

The act of imagination, which is the poem, becomes a bridge to a new state of consciousness, a unitive state to which the reader implicitly assents. The organic process which results in this act is one of assimilation and regeneration. The appeal of the poem is to the reader's own imagination, and its goal is the liberation of the reader from previous precepts and

preconceptions into the mythic realm of the creative imagination, where he can perceive spiritual illuminations, shining
with a morality essentialized from experience directly, and
begin to move toward his own spiritual articulations. Thus
the poem is not only a "chord" upon which to play the
"major themes of human speculation-love, beauty, death,
renascence,"[22] but also a celebration of the power of the
imagination, the harp that engenders the chord, and hence a
celebration of the life and act of the imagination. The dream
of act is the dream that the poet-persona will, in the life of
his particular imagination, be able to unite diverse materials,
reach a state of unity and absolute innocence, symbolized by
Atlantis, and then cast a "mythic spear," meaning write the
poem, *The Bridge*, that will urge others (the audience) to the
same kind of activity, the same kind of life, that engendered
the poem. It is within this context that *The Bridge*, Crane's
epic of the modern consciousness, must be described.

CHAPTER 2

Structure and Style in *The Bridge*

> It all comes to the recognition that emotional dynamics are not to be confused with any absolute order of rationalized definitions; ergo, in poetry the *rationale* of metaphor belongs to another order of experience than science, and is not to be limited by a scientific and arbitrary code of relationships either in verbal inflections or concepts.[1]

The Bridge is a record, a "history" ("Atlantis"), which simultaneously renders and defines the process by which the poet becomes empowered to act, to embody his truth in an artifact, the poem itself. It is a dramatic narrative of the life of the imagination struggling to give form, and thereby meaning, to its experience of the world. Accordingly, the structure and style of the poem derive from and bear witness to the poet's commitment to the values of the living imagination. Crane's comments on the problem of writing a history of the discovery and exploration of the "body" of the continent (the subject matter of the first half of *The Bridge*) reveal this commitment.

> It seemed altogether ineffective from the poetic standpoint to approach this material from the purely chronological angle—

beginning with, say, the landing of "The Mayflower," continuing with a resume of the Revolution through the conquest of the West, etc. One can get that viewpoint in any history primer. What I am after is an *assimilation of this experience,* a more organic panorama, showing the continuous and living evidence of the past in the inmost vital substance of the present.[2] (Italics mine.)

This rendering of past experience in terms of the present[3] is but one aspect of the poet's movement through various stages of history and states of consciousness toward a formal integration of his "modern consciousness" in the perception-creation of the Bridge, the "one arc synoptic" of the process. That Crane believed the various sections of *The Bridge* to be unified within themselves and with each other is certain:

For each section of the poem has presented its own unique problem of form, not alone in relation to the materials embodied within its separate confines, but also in relation to the other parts, *in series,* of the major design of the entire poem. Each is a separate canvas, as it were, yet none yields its entire significance when seen apart from the others. One might take the Sistine Chapel as an analogy.[4]

The structural principle of the poem, then, is bifurcated. Each section renders the achievement of the imagination's unitive truth, or the failure to achieve it. And the sections *in series* render the poet's movement through states of consciousness (note Crane's reference to the "body" of the continent) toward his own unitive act, the perception-creation of the Bridge. It is this latter act which liberates the poet into the mythic realm of the creative imagination, symbolized by Atlantis, in which state he is empowered to cast a "mythic spear" of his own, i.e., to write *The Bridge.* The poem, in turn, becomes itself a Bridge for the reader, for the poet's people, whereby they too may cross over to that state of consciousness symbolized by Atlantis.

The process by which the poet comes to "know" and finally embody the experience of his knowledge is similar to the process by which, in Crane's poetic theory, a poet comes to "know" anything which he wishes to incorporate in a poem. This organic process is one of recognition, assimilation and regeneration, and in *The Bridge* is accomplished by having the fictional poet encounter, respond to, and assimilate, then move beyond the experience embodied in each section of the poem. The process is one of self-knowledge, more so than knowledge of a culture. The different locales and times of the poem, though they do vaguely span the history and breadth of America, have their main value in terms of the poet's developing consciousness, his movement toward the recognition of the "intrinsic Myth" ("Atlantis") of the intuitive imagination. As Crane noted, the relationship of the poet to temporal or spatial locale is incidental to the creative act that is his desideratum:

> I put no particular value on the simple objective of "modernity." The element of the temporal location of an artist's creation is of very secondary importance; it can be left to the impressionist or historian just as well. It seems to me that a poet will accidentally define his time well enough simply by reacting honestly and to the full extent of his sensibilities to the *states of passion, experience and rumination* that fate forces on him, first hand. He must, of course, have a sufficiently universal basis of experience to make his imagination selective and valuable. His picture of the "period," then, will simply be a by-product of his curiosity and the relation of his experience to a postulated "eternity."[5]
> [italics mine]

That the poet's growth must be the fundamental act of the poem is evident from the fact that the Bridge, which after "Proem" does not appear symbolically until the last section, must indeed be, as Tate called it, "a trivial symbol" inadequate to what it must support, unless it is seen as the natural culmination of the series of bridging, unitive acts which have occurred in previous sections of the poem. After all, it is not the Brooklyn Bridge but the symbolic Bridge, the act of the creative imagination, that initiates, capsulizes and crowns the poet's growth.

The poet's movement in *The Bridge* toward Atlantis, his "postulated 'eternity'," parallels the growth of his consciousness toward the recognition of the imagination's unitive power. "Proem" is at once prior and posterior to the rest of the poem, for there the poet prays to a Bridge symbolic of a truth and power he has experienced before ("And we have seen night lifted in thy arms"), and asks that he may experience it again ("Unto us lowliest sometime sweep, descend,/ And of the curveship lend a myth to God.") "Proem," then, is a reflection on an act completed for the purpose of beginning the act again, reenacting it. Hence it is both beginning and end of the circular process rendered in *The Bridge*; or, rather, the end of the process and the beginning of the poetic stage, the act of recording the process.

The subject matter of the first half of *The Bridge* ("Ave Maria" through "Cutty Sark") is the discovery and exploration of the body of the continent. But the subject is the growth of the poet in the wisdom of the flesh, its powers and limitations vis-a-vis the imagination. In "Ave Maria" the fictional poet is physically absent, though in the birth of the first consciousness of America as America (Columbus's discovery and struggle to bring back the "word" of the discovery) his own birth of consciousness is rendered. This birth of consciousness is followed by the poet's emergence from sleep into modern Manhattan, from which he journeys retrospectively through "Copybook" memory and blood memory into his own and the nation's past. "Powhatan's Daughter" renders the poet's pursuit of Pocahontas and liberating love through the body. He achieves physical integration and realizes the power of the flesh through union with Pocahontas in

"The Dance," but sees the failure of this unitive truth to perpetuate itself through the body alone in "Indiana" and "Cutty Sark." Though generated by passion, the imagination's truth cannot be conveyed or transmuted by passion alone.

The subject matter of the second half of *The Bridge* is the exploration of the spirit of the continent (Crane's alternate title for "Cape Hatteras"), and the attempts to embody that spirit in an act of imagination. The subject is the fictional poet's increasing awareness of the limitations of reason and intellect (whose act is scientific, like the invention of the airplane or subway) and the possibilities of the poetic imagination (whose act is the creation of a living art). In "Cape Hatteras" the poet awakes from his reverie of the past into a new "dream of act," a dream of creating an artifact that will embody the truth of the spirit. In place of the false god of gold which offered itself as a static alternative to the truth of the body and passion's regeneration in "Indiana," the poet is faced with the acts of science and modern technology, symbols of the mind's attempt to render inert, or inertly mechanical, the living truth of the spirit. He learns from Whitman to choose "something green" and living, "beyond all sesames of science," as his desideratum. In "Three Songs" and "Quaker Hill" the poet encounters the failure of traditional ideals of love and religion to embody a living truth, but grows in his awareness of the poetic act and construction as the source of the enduring, living artifact. "The Tunnel" renders the poet's own movement through the labyrinth of the mental and mechanical, the mind's possibilities. The death of the intellect is followed by the dropping of "Memory" itself into the waters of the harbor, as the poet has learned and exhausted the possibilities of both body and mind in his quest for the bridging act of the unitive imagination. "The Tunnel" ends with the poet invoking the imagination's power, "O Hand of Fire/ gatherest."

"Atlantis" renders, in a three-fold progression, the poet's perception-creation of the symbolic Bridge, his reflection on the powers of the Bridge as "intrinsic Myth," and his passage from the Bridge to Atlantis (an "attitude of spirit," Crane called it). The Bridge embodies the journey that has preceded it, and it leads "to Thee, O Love." It reveals the unity and harmony of the entire world under the aegis of the love-driven imagination, a revelation symbolized by the reaching of Atlantis. The reaching of Atlantis is for the poet a self-realization of the "intrinsic Myth" of the imagination, and this realization empowers him to perform his final act, the writing of the poem itself, the casting of his own "mythic spear."

That the process of growth, a learning process ("inference and discard" yielding "faith" is the image from "Ave Maria"), is necessary to the poet's ultimate recognition of the symbolic Bridge is stated in "Atlantis."

> Sheerly the eyes, like seagulls stung with rime—
> Slit and propelled by glistening fins of light—
> Pick biting way up towering looms that press
> Sidelong with flight of blade on tendon blade
> —Tomorrows into yesteryear—and link
> What cipher-script of time no traveller reads
> But who, through smoking pyres of love and death,
> Searches the timeless laugh of mythic spears.

The "cipher-script of time" fused by the Bridge is perceived only by the traveller who can see through the "smoking pyres of love and death," the subject matter of art, to the mythic act of creation that is art's true subject,[6] that bears witness to the imagination's "Everpresence." This is the perception that empowers the poet to fulfill his own "dream of act."

Because the subject of *The Bridge* is a process, the values of the experiences rendered in the poem must be derived

from their relationship to that process. Since the process is
one of the development of consciousness, the poet is primar-
ily a "mental traveller," moving through states of consciousness toward the recognition of the imagination's unitive truth.
Values, then, are determined by the role of various phenom-
ena in aiding or threatening the poet's growth of consciousness, advancing or retarding it, illuminating or obscuring its
goal. But this is not to say that some values are good and
others bad in any ethical sense, for as the epigraph to this
chapter declares, "emotional dynamics are not to be con-
fused with any absolute order of rationalized definitions."
Indeed, the unitive vision cannot exclude any experience or
value; rather, it prevails by incorporating and transforming
everything in its creative act. Consequently, Whitman, termed
by the poet the Meistersinger "Of that great Bridge, our
Myth," is praised in "Cape Hatteras" for his "Sea eyes and
tidal, *undenying,* bright with myth!" [italics mine].

Not only the structure but also the poetic style renders
the "incarnate *evidence*" of this process, and thus fulfills its
"Sanskrit charge," revealing the poet's commitment to a living art, one that possesses and is possessed by its own dynamic
vitality. The dramatic narrative of the fictional poet renders
the processive integration, the past with the living present.
And the circular structure of this dramatic narrative allows
the poem to move, not from past to present, but through the
present to the "Everpresence, beyond time," of Atlantis.
Poetic technique concentrates on a similar presence and immediacy, utilizing coalescence and juxtaposition of events
rather than sequential and causal development to render the
continuous and eloquent span of the poem. Coherence is
achieved through metamorphosis[7] and repetition of images
and symbols. As Crane wrote to Waldo Frank:

> Are you noticing how throughout the poem motive and situations
> recur—under modifications of environment, etc.? The organic

substances of the poem are holding a great many surprises for me. . . . Greatest joys of creation.[8]

These "organic substances" include, for instance, the metamorphosis of the Female, symbolic of the love that finally liberates the man of vision into the mythic realm of the imagination, from the Virgin of "Ave Maria" through the fictional poet's own mother and Pocahontas, to the Christian types of Woman ("Eve, Magdalene, or Mary, you?") who are the subjects of "Three Songs" and the "Wop washerwoman" met on the ride through "The Tunnel." Each symbolizes love *sub speciae aeternitatis,* and as symbols, rather than allusions or allegorical figures, they are immediate and living. They have been generated in and through the context of *The Bridge*—their powers and limits, their significance, depend on their integrity with the interior form of the poem itself. Thus they are both structuring devices of the poem and structures within the poem, not so much extra-referential as synecdoches of both the poem and the poetic process. As Crane wrote to Frank, in an exuberant expression of those "greatest joys of creation," conceiving his Columbus: "My plans are soaring again, the conception swells. Furthermore, this Columbus is REAL."[9]

Correlative with Crane's attempt to render the imagination's life through his use of symbolism is the use he makes of allusion. The purpose of the connective act, the making of a bridge, is, as delineated in "Proem," to "lend a myth to God." Within *The Bridge* the unitive act occurs (or significantly fails to occur, thereby affirming itself dialectically through negation) under various modifications of environment; thus the "God" it seeks takes on different names. Columbus "merges the wind in measure to the waves" and thereby makes the ocean a bridge which reveals to him the truth of the "incognizable Word/ Of Eden and the enchained Sepulchre," the "sounding heel" of "Elohim." Maquokeeta, the Indian shaman, performs a dance that makes him a living bridge between heaven and earth, and thereby proves to his own satisfaction the truth of the Indian myth of the "Largesse" of the "immortal" Earth-Mother goddess Pocahontas, she who is "virgin to the last of men." The insufficiency of the Christian myth to God is evident in "Three Songs," where the poet laments the inefficacy of the symbolic types of Woman and the loss of "God—your namelessness." And finally, it is the "intrinsic Myth" of the Bridge that connects the poet with "Deity's young name." Thus the poet moves toward the Bridge, the imagination's "steeled cognizance," by experiencing and assimilating earlier definitions. The allusions to the myths of other times, "other calendars" or other "indexes of night" ("Atlantis"), are not merely decorative acknowledgements of a "useless archaeology."[10]

Crane's purpose is not to acknowledge a tradition but to shape and present the living stuff of the imagination in whatever terms are organically justified:

> The great mythologies of the past (including the Church) are deprived of enough facade to even launch good raillery against. Yet much of their traditions are operative still—in millions of chance combinations of related and unrelated detail, psychological reference, figures of speech, precepts, etc. These are all a part of our common experience and the terms, at least partially, of that very experience when it defines or extends itself.[11]

The poet lives in and through other *personas* in the poem, as he moves through layers of consciousness, descending like the "bedlamite" of "Proem" through old selves and skins toward recognition of and communion with his own vital matrix, the "kingdoms naked in the trembling heart" ("Ave Maria"), from which he can act. The journey is truly difficult, as Crane knew, for the known must give way to and be reborn in the unknown, the new. Thus the allusions to old mythologies are actually made to celebrate the present Myth of the Bridge, made to come alive as elements of the poet's experience of himself and of the personality of life.

The symbolic Bridge is the organic construct by which the poet unites time and space (puts "The serpent with the eagle in the leaves" of his poem) in one unitive act that condenses "Tomorrows into yesteryear." The poem's subject is itself, how the imagination prepared itself to act, to write the poem. The play on the word "leaves" at the conclusion of the poem, recalling Whitman's similar cosmic pun in *Leaves of Grass,* is the culmination of a series of references to the poet's task of translating the imagination's truth into the written medium. That the poem's subject is, finally, itself, how it came to be created, is suggested in the poet's scorn of "copybook" writing in "Van Winkle," his efforts to reach Pocahontas "beyond the print that bound your name" in "The River," his reception of inspiration from Whitman's living poetry in "Cape Hatteras," and his ecstatic recognition of the Bridge as a "Choir, translating time" into the "multitudinous Verb" of the imagination's "Everpresence" in "Atlantis." The device of paradox is one of the linguistic constructions by which the poet uses his medium to yoke opposites and render the implicit but vibrant harmony of things logically irreconcilable. The Bridge itself is described in paradox: "implicitly thy freedom staying thee!" And the significance of the Bridge's freedom-in-stasis, its "motion-in-repose," in "Proem," is indicated as being its implicit comment on the possibilities of attaining the reconciliation of "things irreconcilable," of achieving a similar unitive yet vital state: "Vibrant reprieve and pardon thou dost show." The device of paradox is admirably suited to the rendering of a vital and living art, generating as it does a unitive meaning implicit in the dualities in yokes.

The Bridge of "Atlantis" functions as a sort of perpetual paradox, translating time and the manifold separate voices of time "into what multitudinous Verb the suns/ and synergy of water ever fuse, recast/ In myriad syllables—Psalm of Cathay!"

This unitive act of the Bridge, of bridging, is the Psalm of Cathay, the unceasing song to that unitive state symbolized by Cathay-Atlantis. And it is essentially the same act as that performed by paradox. Indeed, in "Ave Maria" the life of man is defined as a "parable," suggesting not only the riddle of man's existence but also the means by which the riddle is solved, through the creation of the parabola of a Bridge or the paradox of language. The evocation of passion and "synergy" achieved through the use of paradox recalls a statement by Kierkegaard on the nature of paradox: "The paradox is the source of the thinker's passion and the thinker without paradox is like a lover without feeling, a paltry mediocrity."[12] In a real sense the paradox, the linguistic act of bridging, reveals the source of the poet's passion as his poetic imagination in *The Bridge,* and is thus instrumental in rendering the living act of imagination.

Another important technique in the rendering of the imagination's efforts to fuse and thereby recreate experience within the confines of the printed medium is the use of etymology. Crane's predilection for the dictionary, his constant search for unique words and a uniqueness of words, is well known. Throughout *The Bridge* Crane employs words in their radical sense, drawing upon their etymology to suggest significant ambiguity, to force latent meaning to the surface. This important tool in the conquest of consciousness is used effectively in such words as "bedlamite" ("Proem"), "threshold" ("Proem"), "chevron" ("Ave Maria"), "Sabbatical" ("Van Winkle"), "dorsal" ("Cape Hatteras"), to reveal in the present the living evidence of the past and of the Word, in terms of language itself.

The language of the poem, justly praised for its sensuous and concrete qualities, is equally important in rendering the continuous and eloquent span. Questions, for instance, are frequent: not "why" questions, which would suggest causes, but "how" questions, which reflect the poet's desire to accept and emulate new patterns, new shapes, changes for their own sake. Exclamations punctuate the poem as intensity of feeling becomes a thematic principle in an organic process concerned with growth and regeneration. Static, abstract statements, propositional dicta, scientific "theorems sharp as hail" ("Cape Hatteras") are anathema to the organic process, and used within the poem as in "Quaker Hill," only to suggest a state of mind which is antagonistic to the imagination's growth.

One of the keys to an appreciation of Crane's use of language to construct his "architectural art" is the recognition of the generative function and thrust of what Crane called his "logic of metaphor."

> As to technical considerations: the motivation of the poem must be derived from the implicit emotional dynamics of the materials used, and the terms of expression employed are often selected less for their logical (literal) significance than for their associational meanings. Via this and their metaphorical interrelationships, the entire construction of the poem is raised on the organic principles of a "logic of metaphor," which antedates our so-called pure logic, and which is the genetic basis of all speech, hence consciousness and thought-extension. [13]

Defending his use of this technique in one of his poems, Crane explains a particular image in this way:

> Although the statement is pseudo in relation to formal logic—it *is* completely logical in relation to the truth of the imagination, and there is expressed a concept of speed and space that could not be handled so well in other terms. [14]

That this use of language depends for its effect on the receptivity of the reader's imagination is clear:

It implies (this *inflection* of language) a previous or prepared receptivity on the part of the reader. . . .

If one can't count on some such bases in the reader now and then, I don't see how the poet has any chance to ever get beyond the simplest conceptions of emotion and thought, of sensation and lyrical sequence. If the poet is to be held completely to the already evolved and exploited sequences of imagery and logic— what field of added consciousness and increased perceptions (the actual province of poetry, if not lullabyes) can be expected when one has to relatively return to the alphabet every breath or so?[15]

The uses of language to push back the frontiers of consciousness and perception by building an organic construct is Crane's hope and his goal. "Language has built towers and bridges, but itself remains as fluid as always."[16]

Within *The Bridge* the use of the logic of metaphor is abundantly evident. An example is the flow of the River toward the Gulf rendered at the end of "The River." The River proceeds, accumulating and reworking all the diverse elements that "feed it timelessly," toward union with the Gulf, and it is this passionate junction of Time and Eternity that carries the poet into the next section of the poem and the timeless "mythic" land of "The Dance." The thrust of the River, then, is toward a new, mythic state of consciousness, and the movement of this thrust is internal and inferential, fusing elements beneath its surface, building "bridges" below the level of concepts. The River's force and flow, "O quarrying passion, undertowed sunlight," moves both linearly and internally, as it "flows within itself, heaps itself free," until:

> The River lifts itself from its long bed,
> Poised wholly on its dream, a mustard glow
> Tortured with history, its one will—flow!
> —The Passion spreads in wide tongues, choked and slow,
> Meeting the Gulf, hosannas silently below.

Here in the concluding lines of "The River" are examples of many of Crane's poetic techniques, including the logic of metaphor. The allusions to the Christian Passion and Atonement heighten the significance of the fusion of Time and Eternity in terms of the poet's experience of that fusion. The paradox of "hosannas silently below" suggests the implicit yet powerful impulse to praise the necessary but painful union. The logic of metaphor is evident in such images as that of the River "poised wholly on its dream," which suggests simultaneously the lifting of the River upwards and the balancing of the River for one moment "wholly" (with a pun on "holy") on its heaping "dream," its will to flow. Or consider the "mustard glow" of the River's "undertowed sunlight," earlier imaged as "ochreous and lynx-barred." The emotion of the passage is perhaps illogical (how could the River be at once a dreamer and poised on top of its dream? how can mustard "glow"?), but is "completely logical in relation to the truth of the imagination."

Further, the effect of the passage is not impressionistic but constructive, not imitative but creative, evocative of a new state of consciousness. The clustering of images and metaphors in the passage does not allow for mere retinal registration or "psychological stimulation,"[17] but forces the reader's sensibility in a predetermined direction which must be imaginatively rather than rationally assented to. As Crane noted about another of his poems: "A poem like Possessions really cannot be technically explained. It must rely (even to a large extent with myself) on its organic impact on the imagination to successfully imply its meaning."[18] The poetry renders itself immediately and vitally, by organic impact on the imagination rather than the impressionistic retina, what Crane called "the readiest surface of consciousness, at least relatively so."[19] And it is accepted insofar as the audience has "an active or inactive imagination as its characteristic."[20] The poet, of course, is liable to error and excess in this process, but as Crane noted, "it is part of the poet's business to risk not only criticism—but folly—in the conquest of consciousness."[21]

Crane's appeal to the reader's imagination in the conquest of consciousness is indicative both of his goal and his method in *The Bridge*. Both structure and style in his long poem are engaged in the "actual (physical) representation of the incarnate *evidence*" of the poet's recreation of the world, his creation of a self-sufficient structure. Accordingly, a critical reduction of the poem to ideas and abstractions about the world to some extent begs the question. A recent critic formulated the problem:

> A work of art encountered as a work of art is an experience, not a statement or an answer to a question. Art is not only about something; it is something. A work of art is a thing *in* the world, not just a text or commentary *on* the world.[22]

The protean nature of *The Bridge* is not conducive to argument; rather, it invites description, analysis, illumination of the poem's structural relationships and the values inherent in those relationships. The proof of Crane's accomplishment is in *The Bridge*; there his imagination displays its true poetic intentions, and his craft its worth in effecting them. Let the poetic theory serve as orientation, as map in finding and charting the structure, and the values implicit therein, of Crane's attempt to give form to "the living stuff of the imagination."

CHAPTER 3

Proem

Crane chose an epigraph from the Book of Job to introduce his poem that serves at least two functions. Lucifer's statement precedes the storytelling process in Job, and here it infers that the poem about to begin has itself been preceded by a journey to which the narrative stands as record and exemplum. The story is the act resulting from the journey. Secondly, by alluding to Job at the start of his poem, Crane implies that his epic of the imagination is a theodicy whose diety is as elusive, but as real, as the *deus absconditus* of the Old Testament story. Crane's deity, of course, is the imagination itself, and intrinsic rather than transcendental. The epigraph leads naturally into "Proem," which stands as prelude and icon to the imagination's history, which is recorded in *The Bridge*.

The first image of "Proem" is of the seagull rising from the harbor of Manhattan at dawn, flying up towards the new sun and out towards the ocean, leaving behind the "chained bay waters" and "building high" in its flight "Liberty." Nature is active, providing for man this example of awakening and creative release, making the poet admire and desire it for himself. The spiraling flight draws from him an exclamation-question, "How many dawns," which suggests his wonderful appreciation, his awe, and his own natural urge for a similar release. The image of the gull spiraling up at the sign of the sun, "Shedding white rings of tumult," suggests regeneration, renewal, and subtly associates the gull image with a later one, that of "Time like a serpent"; for here in "Shedding" is the hint of the sloughing off of old skins, old lives and times as well as spaces, of the movement toward life through death and metamorphosis. The gull's activity is architectural, "building high," and the result is "Liberty." As the sun's energies freed the gull from a cold "rippling rest," so the bird's creative flight stirs the poet to dreams of a similar liberating act. Here "Liberty" suggests both freedom and love, for the Statue of Liberty is the first image of the Woman symbolic of liberating Love invoked throughout the poem. The end of the gull's constructive flight is the unitive act of the "inviolate curve," the perfect bridge-like arc to which his "white rings of tumult" have led.

From the vision of the ascending gull the poet's attention turns downward, and the confinement and redundancy of the Manhattan "multitudes" are encountered: dealing in abstractions, "figures to be filed away," they work in the office buildings of the city until elevators "drop" them "from our day." For them the sight of the gull's inviolate curve is "apparitional," deprived of its flesh-and-blood vitality, and in its place are "cinemas, panoramic sleights, the flashing scene/ Never disclosed, but hastened to again." The poet, who saw the gull with his eyes, here "thinks" of the multitudes watching the cinemas, an important acknowledgment of the cleavage between immediate and vital experience and abstract reflection, between life and thought, which the poet must reconcile. These are the two poles of the imagination's existence, the body and the mind, which must first be harmonized if the unitive act is to be completed.

The living but transitory freedom of the gull and the permanent mechanical confinement of the cinemas can be harmonized in the vital structure of the Bridge. This is the model for the poet's act, the construction, a new creation, which binds the antitheses together. "And Thee, across the harbor, silver-paced/ As though the sun took step of thee, yet left/ Some motion ever unspent in thy stride,—/ Implicitly thy freedom staying thee!" Where the gull was urged to flight by the sun, and the office buildings shut out the sun, confining the poet to "thought," the Bridge and the sun are mutually defining. Like musical notes and the staff on which they are set, the sun takes "step" of the Bridge yet leaves "Some motion ever unspent" in its stride. The image foreshadows that of "Atlantis," where the supporting cables of the Bridge are "gleaming staves," The Bridge unites in one living, individual form the sun and steel, the gull and the cinema, the body and the mind. It is not static, but dynamic, evincing "some motion ever unspent" in its "stride," its freedom "staying" it.

An abortive response to the implicit freedom of the Bridge is made by one of the multitudes in the next stanza, as the imagination moves to the problem of applying the freedom evinced in the Bridge to its own life. The "bedlamite" rushes from his "subway scuttle, cell or loft" and leaps from the Bridge while unconcerned motorists continue on their "speechless caravan." His fall is imaged in terms of speech, but this attempt to individuate himself is not an act of despair, but a search for a rebirth, as the etymology of "bedlamite" suggests. Crane's penchant for using words in their radical sense is well illustrated here, for "bedlam" refers both to the famous lunatic asylum in London called Bedlam and to the full name of that abbreviation: the hospital of St. Mary of Bethlehem. Thus the bedlamite is associated not only with insanity but also with Bethlehem and the birth of the Word made Flesh, and while he fails to achieve a similar rebirth here his intentions are evident. His impulse is toward the same sort of freedom, that of the integrity and harmony of the truth of the imagination, which the Bridge evinces. The pathology is clear: "To be drowned in order to be born again—this is the myth of the positive integrative aspect of experiencing truth."[1] The Christian imagery of the poem suggests not the birth of Christ but the recurrent birth of the imagination's word, the continual recreation by bridging of the "multitudinous Verb" of "Atlantis." This use of the Incarnation as image of the creation of the poem further extends to the unification of time and space in one moment, for the act of the imagination puts "the serpent with the eagle in the leaves," joins time and space, just as in Christian tradition the Incarnation and At-onement represent the total unity of time and space in one moment (as witness our dating of time from Christ's birth).

The death by drowning of the bedlamite leads to an affirmation of the Bridge as living, as its "cables breathe the North Atlantic still," suggesting again the enduring and transcendent life of the imagination's act. The sun of noon "leaks" into the city, "Down Wall, from girder into street," a liquid fire, "rip-tooth of the sky's acetylene." The inseparability of creation and destruction in the "rip-tooth" subtly carries on the association of birth through death that surrounded the bedlamite, but with the difference that here the creation is the organic construction, where the vital sun is imaged as the mechanical acetylene torch that shapes, as it were, the city itself, by firing the space around the buildings, ordering them by its light into definite forms. It is the image of architectural construction, the harnessing of life forces in order to make and shape, the flow of the vital on the inanimate that involves both destruction and creation, the act which creates the living Bridge.

In the next four stanzas the imagination reflects on the qualities of the Bridge. It promises a "guerdon" that is "obscure as that heaven of Jews," suggesting the this-wordly quality of the imagination's absolute, like the Jewish heaven-on-earth, a unity and harmonization of the natural, not an escape from it. The "accolade" which the Bridge "bestows" has a similar "anonymity" that "time cannot raise" or, by the pun, "raze." The Bridge "shows" a "Vibrant reprieve and pardon" to the imagination, a living and harmonious freedom from time and death, the same sort of liberation that attracted the bedlamite. Religious imagery describes the Bridge as an object of prayer: "O harp and altar, of the fury fused." It is both the instrument of harmony and the place of sacrifice and worship, the altar, where the power of the imagination is celebrated and made manifest. By joining the symbol of poetry (the harp) and deity in one, the imagination suggests that "God" is really its own mythic truth. In "Terrific threshold of the prophet's pledge" of unity the imagination foreshadows the symbolic union of nature and the machine that occurs under the aegis of the Bridge in "Atlantis," where "the cities are endowed/ And justified conclamant with ripe fields/ Revolving through their harvests in sweet torment." As "prayer of pariah" the Bridge symbolizes the unitive disclosure via visual perception denied the multitudes at the cinemas; as the "lover's cry" it is emblematic of the imagination's appeal for loving unity.

In the next stanza night has fallen, as the vision of the Bridge begets a powerful but implicit desire for speech, and the poet begins to dream of his own action. The Bridge in darkness is beaded by traffic lights "that skim" its "swift/ Unfractioned idiom." The "inviolate curve" of the gull has here become, with an important change, the "Unfractioned idiom" and the "immaculate sigh of stars," emphasizing that the poet's Bridge, *The Bridge*, must be an artifact of words, of poetry, the "multitudinous Verb" that can "condense eternity," The poet remembers that "we have seen night lifted in thine arms," that in the past he has known the power of the act of the imagination to lift darkness into the light; and he prays to this power of the imagination itself, implicit in the Bridge that can unite both the body and the mind in its "Unfractioned idiom."

As "Proem" draws to a close the process by which the poet has moved from the vision of the gull flying toward the sun leaves him under the shadow of the Bridge, waiting. He has moved through the City to the Bridge, from the natural through the mechanical to the imaginative, and he declares that "Only in darkness is thy shadow clear." The season of Christmas is suggested: "The City's fiery parcels all undone,/ Already snow submerges an iron year." And in conjunction with Christmas and the earlier "bedlamite" the waiting of the poet suggests a waiting for an epiphany, a birth, an insight, an awakening from his "dream" of act into the act itself. The paradox of the shadow of the Bridge being clear "only in darkness" suggests that the ultimate reality of the Bridge resides dormant within the poet himself, that he has had to undergo a symbolic blinding of his mental faculties in order to truly assimilate the significance of the Bridge as an active principle in his own consciousness. The organic construct of the act of the imagination is light-ridden, glorious, but the final acceptance of it must be in the dark inarticulate regions of the individual, where it will serve to generate further life and finally lift night into the light again. This is the relationship of the poet persona to the Bridge at the end of "Proem," where he has finally come under the Bridge to wait for it to "sometime sweep, descend/ And of the curveship lend a myth to God." He has come to recognize that the arching curve of the gull and the Bridge's "Unfractioned idiom" embody a truth that is his truth too, that of the life and power of the imagination which lies dormant, like the "prairies' dreaming sod," within him.

Thus, he prays to, invokes, the imagination itself, what Crane called that "power-in-repose" that is "Sleepless as the river under thee." He recognizes that the "Unfractioned idiom" of the arching Bridge is an arc on the spiraling process whereby the imagination's act results from its life and can beget further life. He senses that he himself is the other half of the arching Bridge, and necessary to the unitive act, that the "curveship" of that act finds its source and goal in the life of the imagination itself, that he and the Bridge together form a complete and perfect circle. Thus he introduces *The Bridge*, the record of how the imagination became empowered to create the Bridge to Atlantis, to liberate itself and record that liberation in an act that would become for others a new condition of life, that would generate "new spiritual articulations."

CHAPTER 4

Ave Maria

The subject matter of "Ave Maria" is the struggle of Columbus to return to Europe with the "record" of his discovery of America-Cathay. The epic begins *in medias res* with the explorer in mid-ocean on the return trip. His problem is not discovery, but the bringing back to others of his "truth, now proved." His prayer, "some inmost sob," transforms the threatening ocean into a bridge that unites "Cathay" and Europe. By his act of harmonizing wind and water in one "teeming span" Columbus affirms the unitive nature and "Everpresence" of the deity to whom he prays. And his voyage of discovery, begun with a prophecy of future worlds and new, concludes with a hymn to Elohim and the voyager's own perpetual thrust toward "still one shore beyond desire!"

The subject of "Ave Maria" is the struggle of the American imagination, through its objective-correlative Columbus, to move into consciousness and self-recognition, to "lift night," to bring to light and life "the word" of its discovery, the "truth, now proved" of its own existence. The movement is one of descent from the memory of initial discovery of

Cathay (an "attitude of spirit") into the dark heart of the stormy and immediate situation in which Columbus finds himself, followed by a regeneration, an ascent into light and an assent to the truth of the imagination's accretion-creation of "This turning rondure whole." The structure of "Ave Maria" is that of struggle resolving itself in song, which of course is the structure of *The Bridge* itself.

Within "Ave Maria" Columbus moves from a conscious evocation of remembered people, and the ritual forms of the prayer "Ave Maria" and hymn *Te Deum*, to the affirmation of another, greater, mode of consciousness, that of the creative mythic imagination, which in man emulates the Logos itself, the hidden source of the energies of the universe. Columbus's movement is characterized by a transformation of the mental abstractions into existential realities, vital specifics. The transformation is a stripping process whereby the historical Queen and King and Luis de San Angel, the theological Maria and Deus and Angelus, come down to love, system and music, finding their true being in "kingdoms naked in the trembling heart." This descending movement through memory, reflective consciousness and the sentience of the body finds its counterpart and resolution in the "parable of man," the organic construction of the imagination's "kindled Crown," the circular unitive emblem of those "kingdoms naked." Just as the imagination moves through Columbus's conquest of consciousness to the conquest of the "body of the continent" in "Powhatan's Daughter," so "Ave Maria" initiates the larger movement of *The Bridge* which it itself reflects.

This situation of Columbus at the beginning of "Ave Maria" recalls that of the poet at the end of "Proem," for both "have seen" a truth that they are presently attempting to translate into the reality of a "word." Columbus is trying to bring back the word of his discovery of Cathay, and the poet is trying to write a record of his discovery of Atlantis.

Columbus begins his narrative with the remembrance of
"Luis de San Angel...O you who reined my suit/ Into the
Queen's great heart that doubtful day." A response from the
"Queen's great heart" made possible, literally, the journey of
Columbus, just as the answered prayer to "Madre Maria,"
the "inmost sob, half-heard," calmed the abyssmal ocean.
The Queen is the mediatrix between Columbus and Ferdi-
nand, just as the Virgin traditionally united man and God.
But, as Crane noted in a letter,[1] the "cosmography" and religion of Columbus provide merely the "terms" of "Ave
Maria." The heart is the seat of love and vital center of physical life, the source of the energies that inspire and power the
imagination's activity. In the beginning the sea itself is alive
with "Invisible valves...locks, tendons," like some great
heart, but it is "harsh," and "tests the word" of the initial
discovery. Its power must be harmonized, pacified, if the
word is to survive. Columbus recalls his first sighting of "The
Chan's great continent," when "faith, not fear/ Nigh surged
me witless." He remembers that earlier, more propitious juxtaposition of the ocean's energies and imagination's truth:
"...Hearing the surf near—/ I, wonder-breathing, kept the
watch,—saw/ The first palm chevron the first lighted hill."
This sight is inspirational, the breath of "wonder" that
turned fear to "faith." Yet implicit in this image of the
"first palm" as "chevron" of the "first lighted hill" (note the
emphasis on the "first," the proto-typical) is the descent and
death that must follow if the vision is to be brought back in
a "word." For in the choice of "chevron" the poet invokes
the word's etymological association with the goat of sacrifice
and the tragic note that is the goat's song. Paradoxically the
palm, the tree of life, is linked with the goat of death and sacrifice, suggesting the inseparable union of death and resurrection which Crane uses to image the purifying, atoning, redemptive process of the imagination's activity throughout
The Bridge. The allusion to the atonement of Christ is more

explicit in the later reference to the "incognizable Word/ Of Eden and the enchained Sepulchre," and supports the relationship between this death and the birth of the imagination's "word."

But discovery must be followed by the struggle to bring the word back home, and Columbus's sighting of the palm on the "hill" is followed immediately by a descending motion, that of "lowering." Exactly what is "lowered" is uncertain, but such indefiniteness functions to emphasize the motion itself, the descent that follows the revelation, and which, hopefully, leads to the recording of that revelation in the "word." The voyage of Columbus is associated with the flight of the gull in "Proem," for the Indians greet him and his sailors "crying,/ 'The Great White Birds!'"; and by inference the sighting of the palm on the hill is linked with the gull's ascending flight, both promising liberation and urging the imagination on to further activity. Columbus attempts a birth of the word in the abortive gesture of dropping into the sea a "casque" containing news of his discovery and an unassimilated "record of more," which falls, foetus-like, from "under bare poles." This historically and poetically fruitless attempt ends as mere "pawn" for the sea, and echoes the similarly abortive death of the bedlamite, that "jest" dropped from the "speechless caravan" of "Proem."

Contrasted with the aborted word of the casque and the bedlamite is the vital "inmost sob" which "dissuades the abyss,/ Merges the wind in measure to the waves," and leads to the hymn *Te Deum* at the conclusion of "Ave Maria." The motion of descent continues from the image of the casque being dropped into the water to the image of the "shadow" that "cuts sleep from the heart/ Almost as though the Moor's flung scimitar/ Found more than flesh to fathom in its fall," and the descending rhythm and lengthening vowel sounds of the last line suggest its sense. The descent has become interiorized, moving into the heart of Columbus, threatening that

faith that is "more than flesh," both his Christian faith and
his faith in his vision of Cathay, his "truth, now proved."
But it is at this point that the "inmost sob, half-heard" and
by implication half-spoken, like the "whispers antiphonal"
at the end of "Atlantis," occurs to "dissuade the abyss" and
instigate an outward, upward motion. This "inmost sob"
is the paradoxical cry of joy and pain that heralds the emergence, the birth, of the unitive truth; it is the perfect fusion,
the point of atonement, which precedes the resurrection of
the vital "word." It emanates from the heart, the center of
vitality and love, and moves through the eyes and mouth, the
seat of voice, vision, and system, into the light as music. The
outward, expansive movement proceeds through "Series on
series, infinite—til eyes/ Starved wide on blackened tides,
accrete-enclose/ This turning rondure whole, this crescent
ring." The circle symbolizes the unitive vision that is ac-
creted-created by the upward motion through the eyes and
mouth of that initial "inmost sob," an act that recalls the
gull's constructive upward flight through "white rings of
tumult." And the "inviolate curve" of the gull becomes here
the "crescent ring," the arc on the curvature of the earth
which is now perceived as synecdoche of the whole circle and
will not "forsake our eyes," as did the natural gull. For this
"crescent ring" that bespeaks a "turning rondure whole" is
an organic construction "Sun-cusped and zoned with modu-
lated fire/ Like pearls that whisper through the Doge's
hands." The "hands" suggest a human maker and shaper of
this organic construction, and foreshadow the later "Te
Deum laudamus/ O Thou Hand of Fire." It is not God who is
the maker, though Columbus's "cosmography" terms him so,
but the human imagination itself, the source of the "inmost
sob." And the comparison of the gradually lightening earth
to "pearls that whisper through the Doge's hands" emphasizes the role of the human maker, for it is based on the folk-
myth that pearls take their color and warm glow from con-
tact with human flesh. The source of the circle of unitive

vision is Columbus himself, Crane's prototype of the American imagination, who has embodied his "inmost sob" in the "turning rondure whole," and now proceeds to assent, through his concluding hymn *Te Deum*, to the truth of his imaginative vision.

Between the description of Columbus's struggle with the sea and his hymn of praise occurs a transitional stanza, separated from the rest by asterisks, which functions to modulate the tone and rhythm of the "water-swell" crescendo and prepare for what Crane called "the climacteric vision of Columbus.[2] Columbus has come near to "Palos again,—a land cleared of long war," which was the starting point of his circular journey, and his peace is matched by his freedom as "Dark waters onward shake the dark prow free." His return is heralded by an "Angelus" that "environs the cordage tree," and the image of the "Angelus" suggests that the Annunciation of the birth of the word has been made to Columbus, which of course it has, since it is this "word" that he utters in his concluding hymn. The image also presents a transformation of the earlier image of the "palm chevron," both in the play on the "chevron-environs" sound and in the sense of the change from the tragic to the joyful song of the "Angelus." The descent and death that were necessary to transform the initial vision of Cathay into the uttered word have led to this song of imminent birth ascending round "the cordage tree," and "Ave Maria" moves into the final *Te Deum*.

The concluding section of "Ave Maria" evinces a steady, controlled rhythm, as befits the solemnity of a *Te Deum*, and in this regard contrasts with the earlier description of the turbulent, tumultuous sea, as form has emerged from chaos. The section stands as a song in relation to the first section of "Ave Maria," and, as Crane noted, is "later" in time, and "more absolute and marked," than the first section. The agony of Columbus wrestling with the ocean and himself for mastery of "the word" is done. Here Columbus delivers a measured and harmonious prayer to the Word itself, to the power which enabled him to give birth to his "word" of discovery, and to the process by which he became empowered to do so. Columbus recognizes not only the truth of his particular act of the imagination in calming the sea but also the truth of the unitive nature of the imagination itself, the Logos that is the source of all particular imaginative acts. This is the ultimate revelation, for it means that he has discovered the true source of his being in a power of which he partakes but which endures beyond his particular acts. Thus the imagination recognizes and commits itself to further life and movement, to "still one shore beyond desire."

The concluding section moves from a consideration of the paradoxical nature of "Thou who sleepest on Thyself" and the deity's relationship to man to the recognition of the power of this deity in the world and in the universe itself. It ends with a recognition of the unitive nature of all things in the circle of "thy purpose." The deity of Columbus, who "sleepest on Thyself," is self-supporting and self-regenerating. He is compared to that third world "of water," the ocean which is both "apart" and "athwart lanes of death and birth." This reversal of the usual progression from birth to death suggests the imagination's regenerative process through "all the eddying breath between" these poles of existence. Man is God's "parable," His symbol of the union of physical and spiritual in Columbus's cosmography, as the creative act is the imagination's "parable," its symbolic union of disparate, antithetical elements in the harmonious whole of the song or poem, the "word." And it is this Logos aspect of the deity which Columbus addresses: "Inquisitor! incognizable Word/ of Eden and the enchained Sepulchre." This is the paradox which Columbus must recognize in God and in himself, the seeming contradiction between the God of creation and life and the God of suffering and death, the central mystery of the Christian tradition. The triadic movement from glory through ruin to restoration is not only the process by which Christ redeems the world but also the process by which the man of imagination creates his "word." The inclusive Bridge is only possible after the journey under has been completed. Hence Columbus ends this stanza with an affirmation of that process: "Into thy steep savannahs, burning blue,/ Utter to loneliness the sail is true." The paradox of this process is reflected in the "steep savannahs" and "burning blue," imagery that recalls Whitman's description in "Passage to India" of the voyage that is dangerous "but safe" as the navigator's blood "burns" in his veins—suggesting as Crane himself does that the voyage is internal more than external.

The final three stanzas render Columbus' praise of Elohim's power in terms of nature, of the scientific knowledge of his time, and finally of the synthesis of nature and science in the imagination's unitive act. This progression culminates in the image of the horizon as Elohim's "kindled Crown," the circle encompassing the whole cosmos and harmonizing all elements in its scope, and then settles into the recognition of the ultimate human source of this power: "And kingdoms/ naked in the/ trembling heart—."

In nature the power is manifest as that which "grindest oar, and arguing the mast/ Subscribest holocaust of ships," which destroys and, ambiguously, "Subscribest," underwrites in some inscrutable providential manner, this "holocaust." It not only destroys but "sendest greeting by the corposant,/ And Teneriffe's garnet—flamed it in a cloud,/ Urging through night our passage to the Chan." The purgative nature of fire, and the appearance of God-like power in a flame, recalls the earlier mention of the prophet Isaiah and suggests that his relevance to the process of resurrecting the "word" from a death by fire stems from his image in the Old Testament as the prophet whose lips were cleansed by a burning coal sent from God. Columbus resolves this description of a paradoxical power in the same way Isaiah did, by praising the purgation that leads to truth: "Te Deum Laudamus, for thy teeming span!"

In the next stanza the science of navigation, through the instrument of the compass, bears witness to reason's complementary relationship with the unitive nature of the universe. The compass emulates the process of birth through death, of affirmation through negation, for it is "A needle in the sight, suspended north,—/ Yielding by inference and discard, faith/ And true appointment from the hidden shoal." Through "inference and discard" comes "true appointment," a finding of position by "disposition." The stanza concludes with Columbus's affirmation of this power he cannot see. "This disposition that thy night relates/ From Moon to Saturn in one sapphire wheel:/ The orbic wake of thy once whirling feet,/ Elohim, still I hear thy sounding heel!" That Elohim's creative act should be imaged as a dance not only suggests Crane's appropriate use of the Renaissance notion of the cosmic dance but also initiates a motif of creation imaged as a dance or music which persists throughout the poem: in "The Dance," the epigraph to "Atlantis," and the image of the Bridge as "harp," among other places. The unitive act integrates, embodies, both dancer and dance, as Columbus declares, "Elohim, still I hear thy sounding heel!" It draws within the circle's scope or "scan" or "span" all diverse elements, as the whirlwind fuses all in its motion.

This affirmation of the unitive nature of the universe is followed by a steady, triumphant description of the power of the imagination in the present lifting night. "White toil of heaven's cordons, mustering/ In holy rings all sails charged to the far/ Hushed gleaming fields and pendant seething wheat/ Of knowledge,—round thy brows unhooded now/ —The kindled Crown!" The enlightening act joins nature and knowledge under the aegis of the "kindled Crown," the circle symbolic of the absolute of the imagination, here for Columbus the absolute of Christ the King of the World, the Word risen in glory. This final resurrection signals the liberation of the world, for "acceded of the poles/ And biassed by full sails, meridians reel/ Thy purpose." The earth has been released, sent spinning, given, as Crane hoped he could give his poem, "an orbit or predetermined direction of its own." This "kindled Crown" and the rondure it sets turning is for Columbus what Crane hoped his poems would be for his readers, a bridge evocative of a state of consciousness, a new Cathay. The new state of consciousness for Columbus is the recognition of his own part in the unitive nature of the universe and of the laws of the imagination operative within him. Thus the poem concludes with the imagination recognizing "still one shore beyond desire" and other "kingdoms naked in the trembling heart" which it must still explore. For this recognition the man of imagination praises the source of the purgative fire and the unitive vision, the love-driven imagination itself, "O Thou Hand of Fire."

Thus Columbus comes at the end of "Ave Maria" to the same recognition that the poet came to at the end of "Proem," namely the recognition of the power of the imagination itself that lies beneath and informs all particular acts of imagination, all particular bridges. He comes to realize the regenerative life of the imagination in himself. The use of the circle to symbolize the process by which the imagination unifies all elements within its "primal scan," and by which it begets itself out of itself, leads to the next section of *The Bridge*. There the journey is imaged in the epigraph as a turning of cartwheels at the command of Pocahontas, the symbol of love in the "body of the continent" which Columbus has just discovered and which the poet must now explore.

CHAPTER 5

Powhatan's Daughter

The Bridge moves from the imagination's birth in "Ave Maria" toward its awakening to and exploration and assimilation of the possibilities of passion and the flesh in "Powhatan's Daughter;" here it uses the pragmatic intellect to test the powers and limitations of the body, its first task in the making of an organic construct, in the realization of its dream of act. Its objective-correlative, the poet of the poem, is spurred into action by his hope of union with Pocahontas and the liberating love she symbolizes. From "The Harbor Dawn" to the end of "Indiana" the poet goes through the organic cycle of a lifetime, as he moves across the continent and back in time to an Indian civilization based on nature worship. In a letter Crane discussed this movement.

> The love motif (in italics) carries along a symbolism of the life and ages of man (here the sowing of the seed) which is further developed in each of the subsequent sections of "Powhatan's Daughter," though it is never particularly stressed. In 2 ("Van Winkle") it is childhood; in 3 it is Youth; in 4, Manhood; in 5 it is Age. This motif is interwoven and tends to be implicit in the imagery rather than anywhere stressed.[1]

He assimilates the Indians' knowledge, but learns also (in "Indiana") that the natural energies cannot sustain themselves indefinitely without a structure to support them, that the imagination cannot live or communicate its life through the body alone. The love that inspired it and which it seeks is physical and passionate, but it has a spiritual element as well. But here in "Powhatan's Daughter," as the epigraph suggests, love is "Pocahuntus, a well-featured but wanton yong girle" who displays her naked body in the market place and entices the boys to turn cartwheels with her "all the fort over." Thus begins what Crane called the exploration of "the body of the continent."

1. The Harbor Dawn

Writing to Otto Kahn about the first section of "Powhatan's Daughter" Crane noted that "this legato, in which images blur as objects only half apprehended on the border of sleep and consciousness, makes an admirable transition between the intervening centuries."[2] It is a bridge between the "climacteric" vision of Columbus, a conclusion, and a new beginning, heralded by the emergence of the poet himself into consciousness from his "waking dream." Objects "only half apprehended" mark this synesthetic interpenetration of water and land, this passage from the ocean of Columbus to the body of Pocahontas, as "The Harbor Dawn" limns the formless but gestating and potentially harmonious materials with which the imagination must work.

An examination of "The Harbor Dawn" reveals its structural parallels with "Ave Maria," always, of course, under modifications of environment, etc. In "The Harbor Dawn" the poet rests between sleep and consciousness, as "a tide of voices—/...meet you listening midway in your dream." At this "midway" point he resembles Columbus floating "between two worlds"; and, indeed, the poet's state is imaged as a watery "pillowed bay" where voices come in a "tide." The quest motif of "Ave Maria" is continued here in the subtle allusions to Ulysses and his odyssey, specifically in the images of the "sirens," the "Cyclopean towers across Manhattan waters" and "The sun, released." This submerged metaphor linking the imagination's life with the quest of the hero, culminates in the explicit reference to Jason and the Argonauts in the "Atlantis" section. The imagination's shaping power, imaged at the end of "Ave Maria" as a "Hand of Fire," is here relaxed in sleep and dream. Appropriately for this "sowing of the seed," the hands are those of lovers in mutual embrace, as "your hands within my hands are deeds," of both trust and action, whose effects are not immediately known. The hand as maker, shaper, creator, symbolizes the creative activity of the imagination; and here in "The Harbor Dawn" the hands suggest the first coupling of materials, the physical prelude to creation.

In both "Ave Maria" and "The Harbor Dawn" this love-motif moves through natural passion to human love: the lovers' union is prepared for by an imaging of random and unfruitful coupling in nature. The harbor fog is a "blankness," and "Somewhere out there...steam/ Spills into steam, and wanders, washed away/ —Flurried by keen fifings, eddied/ Among distant chiming buoys—adrift." The funereal associations of the accompanying "keen fifings" suggest the abortive motions of natural energy unconverted by the imagination, recalling the bedlamite and the initial "bewilderment" of Columbus, preparing for the dying passion of the River. The imagination must turn the vital energy of nature to human purposes, as it here moves from the harbor to the poet's room, where the fruitful and loving union occurs.

The imagination's transforming activity is imaged in the distillation of the steam that "eddied/ Among distant chiming buoys—adrift" into the dawn which the eyes of Pocahontas "drink" while "a forest shudders in your hair!", an obvious image of sexual consummation. This water cycle results in the reproduction in human and potent form, like the sperm of the poet-lover here, of the abundant natural energies that can be made to beget further life. Here the distillation of the harbor fog by the "sky's/ Cool feathery fold" leads to the symbolic birth of the sun which leads the poet to his lover Pocahontas and possession of the body's wisdom.

"The Harbor Dawn" concludes as did "Ave Maria," with the suggestion of beginning rather than finality, with an impetus onward, as the imagination continues to grow and discover itself. That a conception has occurred is suggested both in the description of the lovers' union and the subtler image of the "mistletoe of dreams," which recalls the Christmas season, the "bedlamite," and Christianity's Incarnation. The image of "still one shore beyond desire" which concluded "Ave Maria" is here echoed in the disappearance of the star, "As though to join us at some distant hill," which "Turns in the waking west and goes to sleep." The woman of the poet's dream has vanished, but there is the promise of her future appearance if the imagination can move beyond time and space, "the world dimensional," into the mythic world of "The Dance."

2. Van Winkle

"Van Winkle," the second section of "Powhatan's Daughter," continues the movement backward in time and westward in space begun in "The Harbor Dawn," as well as the poet's growth through childhood and the "ages of man." The importance of time is evident in the title itself, which invokes the American legend of the man who slept for twenty years, waking to find himself "not here/ nor there." As Crane described it, Van Winkle functions as "the 'guardian

angel' of the journey into the past."[3] The past of continent
and childhood are here connected by the fact that as a
schoolchild the poet "walked with Pizarro in a copybook,/
And Cortes rode up, reining tautly in." The breakdown of
chronological time and temporal suspense, characteristic of
the imagination's infant state in "The Harbor Dawn," carries
into the childhood of "Van Winkle," as music fills the air
while the poet perambulates the surface of land and "copybook" memory on "gold arpeggios," preparing for the descent into "blood memory" and the sexual initiation of "The
Dance." "Van Winkle" evinces a closed form, beginning and
ending with the same stanza, suggestive of the poet's relationship to the materials his imagination must revitalize: they are
the schoolboy's unassimilated copybook records, to be mem-
orized but not possessed. And the interspersion of italicized
stanzas of nursery-rhyme rhythm maintains the force of the
poet's initial injunction to "Listen! the miles a hurdy-gurdy
grinds—/ Down gold arpeggios mile on mile unwinds." The
hurdy-gurdy music encourages the surface impressions and
associations of "memory, that strikes a rhyme out of a box,/
Or splits a random smell of flowers through glass," as the
imagination emulates Van Winkle's movement out of the
present, becoming "time's truant" as "The grind-organ says
...Remember, remember."

The initial image of "Van Winkle" is one of transformation
as well as transition, and thereby sets the pattern for the rest
of this section: "Macadam, gun-grey as the tunny's belt,/
Leaps from Far Rockaway to Golden Gate." It recalls the
description of the Bridge "Vaulting the sea, the prairies'
dreaming sod" in "Proem," and continues the connecting
of past and present, East and West, which is the goal of
"Powhatan's Daughter." The movement from the sea of "The
Harbor Dawn" to the land of "Van Winkle" is imaged as a
shifting of energy, the transformation of the fish's grey belt
into the macadam over which the poet will move through the

land. The living and "leaping" bridge of macadam that results from this transformation of energy is one of the poem's many synecdoches of the Bridge itself.

The theme of transformation established in this initial image continues throughout. Past and present blend in the reverie evoked by the hurdy-gurdy music, as the poet remembers "Times earlier, when you hurried off to school./ It is the same hour though a later day." The measuring of time by the sun's diurnal circuit rather than linear motion from past to present emphasizes the regenerative nature of the imagination's life, whose time perception resembles the ancient symbol of the snake eating its tail, turning in a never-ending (or beginning) circle. The source and goal of the imagination's life is an "Ever-presence, beyond time" ("Atlantis"). Van Winkle, of course, is a perfect symbol for the imagination at this stage of its life, for he has seen urban Broadway transformed from a "Catskill daisy chain in May."

The transformation of fleeting reminiscences of the poet's past into major symbols of experience later in *The Bridge* provides another example of the imagination's regenerative process. The stoning of "young/ Garter snakes under...And the monoplanes/ We launched—with paper wings and twisted/ Rubber bands," both cryptic shorthands of memory here, are, in "The River" and "Cape Hatteras," transformed into major symbols of experience. Similarly, the poet's memory of "the whip stripped from the lilac tree/ One day in spring my father took to me" and of "the Sabbatical, unconscious smile/ My mother almost brought me once from church/ And once only, as I recall" are metamorphosed forms of the suffering and death (in the "whip" of "lilac") and liberation through love (the "Sabbatical," meaning liberating, "unconscious smile") which are necessary to the imagination's act. The evanescent smile, especially, reminds us that the poet's childhood is unredeemed at this stage of the journey. As if sensing this the poet (now fused with Van Winkle, Crane tells

us) tucks the newspaper, the "Times," under his arm and descends to the subway that will carry him to the River and beyond, into the "timeless" and mythic realm of "The Dance."

3. The River

In "The River" the imagination, via the poet, moves beyond the memories of its own and the nation's childhood to
a fuller exploration of the body of the continent and its own
youthful energies. The River is, as Crane called it, "a great
River of Time," and its thrust, its passion, is for a release
from time into eternity. This is its "dream," and it is similar
to the imagination's own dream of act. The structure of "The
River" is triadic. The three divisions deal with, respectively,
the machine and mechanical rhythms, the organic and the
diurnal and seasonal rhythms of nature, and, finally, the integration and harmonization of these opposites in the "great
River of Time" itself, which is imaged as the final measure of
the mechanical and organic tributaries. The formal aspects of
the poetry of these three sections render their relationship to
the imagination's attempt to unite and harmonize. The "telegraphic night" of the machine is an incantatory series of jum-
bled images and broken phrases, what Crane called "the strident impression of a fast express rushing by."[4] The wander-
ing of the tramps across the country, and of the poet through
his recollections of youth, has a "steady pedestrian gait."
The final section, where train and tramps merge with the
River, is a poetry of convoluted rhythms, language thickened
with puns and paradox, as the River "flows within itself"
until it "spreads in wide tongues, choked and slow," meeting
the Gulf with "hosannas silently below." This final suffering
is "The Passion" generated from the River's efforts to unite
and harmonize in "its one will" the conflicting rhythms that

feed its "flow," its life and movement toward and beyond the fatal union with the "Gulf."

Various themes and motifs are clustered around this triadic structure. The machine is associated with all the accoutrements of the rational mentality: abstractions, such as clocks and the printed word, an urge to power through dominance rather than assimilation and loving union, a predisposition to logical reflection rather than intuitive feeling. The organic is associated with the body and the body's vitality, with Pocahontas herself, the body of the continent, who exists "beyond the print that bound her name." Neither machine nor land, urban nor pastoral, man nor woman, is in isolation self-sustaining or replicating; thence, though seeming opposites, they depend on one another for their own generation and regeneration, and this relationship, this antagonism, must be bridged. In order that the imagination may realize its "Everpresence," it must first overcome the mind's threatening, segregative assumptions about time and space. The purpose of this destruction of absolute, or classical, time in "The River" is similar to the purpose of the destruction of absolute space in "Cape Hatteras," and of absolute simultaneity throughout the poem. As Crane knew and felt, the classical rationalist framework that supported these assumptions had been seriously questioned by the formulation of the Relativity Principle (if not by something more mundane, like the cinema or the light bulb). Hence he images the failure of reason and passion to achieve in isolation the unitive truth which he seeks, and then posits the imagination, which Wallace Stevens called "the sum of our faculties,"[5] as the synthesizing, bridging element emulative of and capable of attaining to the love that is the foundation of his universe, the source and end of spiritual articulations.

"The River" opens with the "telegraphic night" of the subway-express train speeding across the country. In a letter on this section, Crane wrote:

the subway is simply a figurative, psychological "vehicle" for transporting the reader to the Middle West. He lands on the railroad tracks in the company of several tramps in the twilight. The extravagance of the first twenty-three lines of this section is an intentional burlesque on the cultural confusion of the present—a great conglomeration of noises analogous to the strident impression of a fast express rushing by.[6]

The "telegraphic night" that introduces "The River" represents a powerful shift from "Van Winkle," where "space is filled with the music of a hand organ and fresh sunlight" and the urban and pastoral motifs intermingle in the figure of Van Winkle, for in this express-train confusion, space is seen through "windows flashing roar," and the "EXpress makes time like/ SCIENCE" in this exercise of the Faustian demiurge that subverts and parodies the pastoral "as you like it ...eh?" The process of mental abstraction associated with science is subtly caught in the "EXpress," and "WE HAVE THE NORTHPOLE/ WALLSTREET AND VIRGIN BIRTH WITHOUT STONES OR/ WIRES OR EVEN RUNning brooks connecting ears." Here words are dissociated from things and made murderously "breathtaking" rather than inspiring. The threat to the unitive imagination is suggested in the ironic exclamation at such abstractions: "can you/ imagine." The music of "Van Winkle" that urged the poet to "remember" has become a cacophony of dismemberment. A "brother" is just a "patent name on a signboard," another example of the extreme isolation of word and thing, mind and body, wrought by the Faustian mentality of "Thomas/ a Ediford." The mechanical repetition of disjointed images never unified recalls the "panoramic slights" of the "flashing scene,/ Never disclosed" which drove the bedlamite to the Bridge in "Proem." The association of synthetic words, "Tintex—Japalac—Certain-teed Overalls," with the product-oriented methodology of "SCIENCE—COMMERCE" further suggests the mental tendencies that threaten, perhaps fatally, the shining "multitudinous Verb" of the Bridge. This failure of the "Twentieth Century Limited," science's supreme fiction, to satisfy man is imaged as the failure to "feed" him, a metaphor of the act of nourishing the imagination throughout the poem. Here the train "roared by and left/ three men, still hungry on the tracks," the hoboes, pariahs of the machine-age who roam the land by rail. It is finally the River itself that swallows the "trainmen" and hoboes who "feed it timelessly."

Crane linked the hoboes of the second part of "The River" with the early pioneers moving into "interior after interior" toward the "pure savage world" of the Indians:

> The rhythm settles down to a steady pedestrian gait, like that of wanderers plodding along. My tramps are psychological vehicles also. Their wanderings as you will notice, carry the reader into interior after interior, finally to the great River. They are the left-overs of the pioneers in at least this respect—that their wanderings carry the reader through an experience parallel to that of Boone and others. I think I have caught some of the spirit of the Great Valley here.[7]

This simple nature, significantly, exists "under a world of whistles, wires and steam," beneath the modern "Iron Mountain" which science and commerce have constructed. The imagination is searching through the land of the continent and the poet's own recollections of a time when both he and the hoboes were "holding to childhood like some termless play" for Pocahontas. And in this second part of "The River" he grows beyond the "Strange bird-wit, like the elemental gist/ Of unwalled winds" which the hoboes "offer," a type of knowledge in which "Time's rendings, time's blendings" are construed "As final reckonings of fire and snow." This ascribing of change to the elemental forces, in a passive, even fatalistic fashion that sets the "unwalled winds" above any human control, is not the philosophy of the poet who, in "Atlantis," compares himself to "Jason...still wrapping harness to the swarming air!"

The contrast between the scientific and organic in terms of their methods of measuring time is presented in the first stanza of this second section: "Keen instruments, strung to a vast precision/ Bind town to town and dream to ticking dream./ But some men take their liquor slow—and count/ —Though they'll confess no rosary nor clue—/ The river's minute by the far brook's year." The difference between time as mathematical abstraction from natural motion and time as accumulation and growth is obvious here; but what is more important in terms of the poem itself is the fact that this organic measure of time is, like the hoboes, closer to the process of assimilation and integration by which the imagination grows and acts. The theoretical intellect abstracts from the change of the universe its concept of time, and in so doing removes change and process from the growth and vitality that underlie and support the human mind itself, committing what Whitehead termed the Fallacy of the Misplaced Concrete. Life, and man, then become products of the mind's abstractions, rather than processes, and art must be a product too. The affinity of the organic concept of time with the imagination's life is suggested in the image of the "rosary," where the series of prayers begins and ends with the crucifix, symbol of the unitive Atonement of Christ.

The hoboes "touch something like a key perhaps," for "they know a body under the wide rain." The body is Pocahontas, symbolic of the land of the red, white and blue U.S.A., "Snow-silvered, sumac-stained or smoky blue." They are "wifeless or runaway," and "Possessed, resigned," to the necessity that they "forever search/ An empire wilderness of freight and rails" for her "yonder breast;" but at least they know that she lives "Past the valley-sleepers, south or west." The poet too has a desire that urges him "past the circuit of

the lamp's thin flame." He is even closer to Pocahontas than
the hoboes, for where they knew her "without name" he has
"dreamed beyond the print that bound her name" in his desire for union. The poet recognizes as "Dead echoes" the
mere printed "copybook" possession of history, of the "red-
skin dynasties that fled the brain." In "The Dance" the margin notes affirm that the true knowledge of Pocahontas must
come through "blood remembering" rather than this ineffec-
tual "brain" remembering.

The next stanza is both a summary of the antagonisms and
a preparation for their assimilation in the descent of the
River into the Gulf. The "old gods of the rain lie wrapped in
pools...Under the Ozarks, domed by Iron Mountain," attended by "eyeless fish" who must "curvet a sunken fountain" to "re-descend with corn from querulous crows." The
imprisoning "Iron Mountain," a spatial parody of the Bridge
that domes and, by a pun, "dooms" the "old gods" to an
"eyeless' existence is associated with the "iron dealt cleavage" that science and the machine have wrought, separating
present from past, mind from body. The sunken fountain
suggests the containment of the imagination and prepares for
the poet's return to its source in the "Appalachian Spring"
of "The Dance," a return necessary to the possession of the
"old gods" and the power of their myth of the body.

The passage through the "telegraphic night" and the
"dream" of the hoboes is signalled by the appearance of
"Pullman breakfasters" who "glide glistening steel/ From
tunnel into field—iron strides the dew—/ Straddles the hill,
a dance of wheel on wheel." Dawn, breakfast and early morning "dew" accompany a new movement within "The River,"
as the poet approaches the Mississippi. He has reconciled the
mechanical and organic rhythms here in a sort of *concordia
discord*, "a dance of wheel on wheel" that still falls short of
the imagination's desire for wheels within wheels (recall
Elohim's "orbic wake"). Now he is ready to descend with the

River to a final destruction of time and a purification of all
desires to locate the imagination's "Everpresence" solely in a
temporal realm. The poet dies to this desire in order to be reborn beyond time, into myth; he emulates the "bedlamite"
in this death by drowning, seeking eventual individuation and
liberation.

The River is masculine, smelling of "musk" and murmur-
ing of *"Memphis Johnny, Steamboat Bill, Missouri Joe,"*
songs of rivermen now dead. It is fed by the trainmen too,
the "Sheriff, Brakeman and Authority" who, in spite of their
efforts to dominate time by stopping it through abstraction,
still "feed the River timelessly." Both the hobo-riverman's
resignation and the Brakeman's resistance fail, as "few evade
full measure of their fate." The figures of "Authority" especially, those who attempt to impose rather than discover
unity, are guilty of hypocrisy as "they smile out eerily what
they seem." The poet notes ironically the imprisoning nature
of this hypocritical, even insane, belief in the superiority of
abstractions, machines and reason to the processes of the universe in his image of the death of a trainman: "I could believe
he joked at heaven's gate—/ Dan Midland—jolted from the
cold brake-beam." The casual, accidental death or, even
worse, the act of divine retribution in the form of a jolt,
undercuts Dan Midland's jocular attitude toward his right to
a place in the heaven of a universe operating on the same
principles that regulated the "Twentieth Century Limited."
The masculine River flows on through the body of the continent, and the hoboes and trainmen move with it, "Down,
down—born pioneers in time's despite." Their death-birth
movement recalls the "lanes of death and birth" in "Ave
Maria," and here the poet is individuated from the others, as
Columbus was from his men, by his recognition of this process. He knows "They win no frontier by their wayward
plight,/ But drift in stillness, as from Jordan's brow." They
are "pioneers" by default, "in time's despite," by virtue of

their feeding of the River of time, which itself has the passion to "flow" onward. It is only the poet, the one who recognizes and engages in this same passion, who is the true pioneer. The image of the men feeding the River as "Grimed tributaries to an ancient flow," with the pun on "grim," recalls the "jest" that fell from the "speechless caravan" streaming across the Bridge ("Proem"). The "bedlamite," in his attempt to give birth to a word by dying, is individuated from the "speechless" others precisely on the basis of his urge toward utterance. Here it is the poet's identification with the River's passion to liberate itself, the failure of speech ("wide tongues, choked and slow"), that individuates him from the hoboes and trainmen who do not share his urge toward the imagination's unitive word.

This unitive urge of the River is poetically rendered through a style characterized by paradox, internal rhyme, and repeated metrical inversions and displacements within a rather closely limited line and stanza form. The effect of such a style is the creation of a sense of turbulence within order, as the imagination tests passion's ability to assimilate and utilize time and space to push beyond to its "postulated eternity." The River assimilates all time in its "alluvial march of days," all space as it "drinks the farthest dale," in its "quarrying passion" that "flows within itself, heaps itself free." Moving through the land, it finally approaches the Gulf, where it dissipates in the "stinging sea." This urge toward unity is imaged as an impetus to realize a dream as "The River lifts itself from its long bed,/ Poised wholly on its dream, a mustard glow/ Tortured with history, its one will— flow!" It is passion's urge toward regeneration and continual life and "flow". The imagination has discovered in passion the regenerative urge of time and space-bound nature, but the River's "dream" holds it only for a moment before it plunges into the Gulf. The image recalls the bedlamite on the Bridge, "Tilting there momently" before his plunge, and indicates via the Christian imagery the possibilities of resurrection associated with this death of the River: "—The Passion spreads in wide tongues, choked and slow, Meeting the Gulf, hosannas silently below." The dissipation of energy and the diffusion of speech are greeted by "hosannas silently below," a paradoxical rendering of the triumph implicit in this death just as it was in Christ's death. As in the Christian Atonement, passion's death unites all time in one moment, and prepares for a resurrection out of time and the imagination's unitive act in "The Dance."

4. The Dance

The union of the poet and Pocahontas occurs in "the primal world of the Indians," beyond the historical and chronological time which was destroyed in "The River." The poet's return to what Crane called the "mythical and smoky soil"[8] leads to the creative act of the Dance itself, which not only unites heaven and earth according to the Indian cosmology but also renders the imagination's assimilation of the potency of the body through the poet's union with the Earth-Mother Pocahontas. The Dance, then, liberates the body into a timeless realm of myth, discovering its enduring innocence (as Pocahontas is "virgin to the last of men") and rendering this truth in the medium appropriate to the flesh, the inarticulate but harmonious dance.

The liberation from time which is signalled by this entrance into the "pure mythical and smoky soil" parallels a liberation of Pocahontas herself as an active inhabitant of the smoky soil. The imagination has moved beyond the print that bound her name in the copybook, to "see her truly," his "blood remembering its first invasion of her secrecy, its first encounters with her kin, her chieftain lover." The poet is simultaneously in the present and the past, for "The Dance" is rendered in the past tense. His blood memory reveals the past which is incorporated within it, and his imagination proceeds to animate it. The "winter king" and the "glacier woman" he squires down the sky at the beginning of this section are generalized types appropriate to the poet's initial remembrance of the inhabitants of the Indian world. But as his blood memory comes into sharper focus, Pocahontas and Maquokeeta are named, individuated, enlivened, as the imagination inspires them with an immediacy and vitality that reaches its climax in the dance itself. There for a short but powerful passage the present tense replaces the past as blood memory gives way to the imagination's "Everpresence." Crane described this reliving of the past: "Not only do I describe the conflict between the two races in this dance—I also become identified with the Indian and his world before it is over, which is the only method possible of ever really possessing the Indian and his world as a cultural factor."[9] At the end of "The Dance" the poet, fused with the Indian shaman Maquokeeta, has freed himself, after having been "assumed into the elements of nature,"[10] to hold "the twilight's dim perpetual throne." In terms of these physical elements which his dance united and harmonized, he has rendered his imagination's "truth."

"The Dance" begins with the poet acknowledging in general terms the cycle of the seasons, the Indian myth of the eternal return to life and spring, and the unitive nature of the physical universe. But accompanying this general recognition are questions of identity and, by extension, of identification: who are the personae of the myth, how can the poet identify with them, integrate their "truth," their life, into his life? The seasonal cycle is imaged in terms of water, as frozen, flowing or re-found "in the autumn drouth," and growth is linked with this water cycle in the pun on "sprouted in "spouted." The "winter king," the un-individuated "swift red flesh," is the figure who brings rain in spring and finds the hidden waters of autumn, recalling the Indian summer. He is at once body and mythical personage, a union of flesh and imagination which the poet himself seeks in this stage of his exploration of the body of the continent; and the winter king's ability to control the flow of water suggests, especially in conjunction with the preceding River of time, that he is capable of controlling Time itself, of liberating the Indian culture from the natural seasonal cycle by evoking both the Indian summer "in the autumn drouth" and the "glacier woman" in the spring. Further, his success in liberating himself from this natural cycle is imaged in his occupation of "the twilight's dim, perpetual throne," where as Crane noted he has been "assumed into the elements of nature,"[11] his life embodied in the realization of imagination's dream of act. He is the one capable of finding the "sunken fountain" and the "old gods of the rain" which in "The River" were "domed by Iron Mountain," and it is his "mineral wariness" which the poet must learn before he can proceed to the dance. Thus the poet re-enacts in the remainder of "The Dance" the role of the "winter king" in these first two stanzas. The process is one of individuation as well as possession, for the poem moves from this general statement of the Indian myth to its particularized reenactment in the dance for Pocahontas, "bride" of love to the imagination's energy. Thus the questions of identity that introduced "The Dance" are answered at the end, and "Who" has become "We" through the imagination's successful assimilation of the truth of the body.

The poet prepares himself for the dance by learning to recognize the unitive impulse in nature itself, in stanzas 6-8, and by recognizing the necessity of death and suffering as prelude to rebirth even in the natural cycle of day and night. Leaving the "village" for "dogwood" is the symbolic act of leaving the known for the unknown, civilization for the wilderness. "Dogwood" suggests both the "Princess whose brown lap was virgin May," i.e., Pocahontas, and the suffering involved in discovering this Princess, for dogwood is traditionally associated with Christ's Passion. The poet learns "to catch the trout's moon whisper" as it leaps out of the "laughing chains" of the water, much as he learned from the soaring gull in "Proem," which is imagistically recalled here; and as the "fleet young crescent" dies "one star, swinging, takes its place, alone," much as the Bridge of "Proem" replaced the gull's "inviolate curve." The notion of the Christian sacrament of the Mass is subtly caught in the imagery of the star "Cupped in the larches" which "bled into the dawn," and suggests the paradox of death preceding rebirth which has occurred elsewhere in the poem. The paradox implicit in a death occurring "immortally" recalls the "perpetual throne" which the star occupies, and suggests the myth of the eternal return which is central to the Indian myth of this section. But the larger associations are implicit in the recognition of the unitive urge of nature itself, the passion of the moth for the moon's light, the trout's leap out of the enchaining waters toward the silver moon, a "whisper" as "antiphonal" as those that answer the poet himself in "Atlantis." He learns to measure this passion in terms of metamorphosis rather than chronology, forgetting "how many hours" in his fascination with a process whereby the river is Pocahontas's "hair's keen crescent running," which gives way to the leaping arc of the trout, then to the "crescent" moon, whose death issues into a "swinging" star that bleeds "immortally" into the dawn. The expansion of arc over arc resolves in the dissolution of the star into the dawn, light into greater light, but the process is perpetual and circular within itself, and the recognition of this natural urge toward unity propels the poet onward in his quest for Pocahontas.

The poet ascends to the "upper flows," where "One white veil gusted from the very top" of the Appalachian Spring.

This image of the "white veil" associates the Spring with the veiled Pocahontas, and with the "glacier woman." The reaching of the Appalachian Spring is the true end of the descent down the River, for here the poet has reached the source of the River of Time itself, and from the Spring he can speed onward to the "Grey tepees" and the dance proper. Crane utilizes the water-cycle as metaphor for this metamorphic and circular process, for the death of the River in the Gulf has become here a birth of the River in the Spring, and the word "gusted" suggests that the River water purified by the "stinging sea" is here precipitated from its sublimated vapor state into pure water—a fine metaphor for the transformational processes of the imagination itself.

The central act of "The Dance" is the union of the Indian's natural world in the dance of Maquokeeta, symbolized by the phenomenon of the whirlwind. The natural phenomenon of the whirlwind is fused with the human dance in a unitive act that measures and liberates both body and spirit: the "cyclone threshes," pulling all elements into its center, employing a process of transformation. The presence of the hidden god of Job and "Ave Maria" is suggested in the image of "the padded foot/ Within" the cyclone, and continues the poem's use of Christian tradition as analogue for the life of the creative imagination. The connection between the whirlwind and the Bridge is rendered in the image of the cyclone purging the heart of the poet himself, drawing "the black pool from the heart's hot root," lifting the darkness.

The Dance of Maquokeeta has the power to reverse time, to "dance us back the tribal morn," or, in the words of "Proem," to "Lend a myth to God." His power resides in his ability to free himself in time, to live "beyond," to be "perpetual" and "immortal;" and his power derives from his allegiance to the unitive act and its mythic implications. The dance, however, is the unitive act of the inspired body, and hence is inferior to the poetic act that seeks to render a "multitudinous Verb."

As in "Ave Maria," the circle is used here as symbol of the unitive act. Maquokeeta is the center of his whirling dance, unifying the entire cosmos in its primal circumference, and finally dancing himself free within the vital matrix itself. The dance-whirlwind not only draws all things to its center, it releases them from the gravity that keeps them earth-bound, setting up a simultaneous ascent-descent movement within the funnel of the cyclone. It becomes a sort of Jacob's ladder, an umbilical cord providing passage from earth to heaven, liberating the dancer in space as the dance liberates him in time. The paradox of simultaneous destruction-creation is a characteristic of the threshing cyclone, as it is of the dancing Maquokeeta, who knows that "death's best," who "casts his pelt" in order that he may live "beyond." The poet, too, is caught up in the dance, "liege/ To rainbows currying each pulsant bone," as he "Surpassed the circumstance, danced out the siege," moved through the destruction to a liberation. The evocation of "rainbows" aptly conveys the liberation that the act of bridging, of surpassing the "circumstance" and the circle, provides, and subtly continues the Christian analogue. His death is imaged as a "dive to kiss that destiny/ Like one white meteor, sacrosanct and blent/ At last with all that's consummate and free/ There, where the first and last gods keep thy tent." Though he had previously risen above the earth, so that "Flame cataracts of heaven in seething swarms/ Fed down your anklets to the sunset's moat," his final act is a loving descent into the world he has ordered in his dance, where he is united and liberated within the circle of his own creation, dwelling in the "tent" kept by the "first and last gods," the alpha and omega of the myth he has just renewed in his dance. He has embodied his and his culture's living truth in a mythical dance, and gained his freedom thereby, performing the quintessential act of "negative capability" by locating his own identity in his imaginative creation.

And yet Maquokeeta's artful ordering of the cosmos is inarticulate, unlike *The Bridge*, which is the verbal record of the poet's own creation of the "multitudinous Verb" of the Bridge. The body of the continent has been explored, and integrated into the imagination via the poet's identification with Maquokeeta in the dance, but Maquokeeta's voice is silent as the poet concludes "The Dance" with his own words. The poet has learned the body's wisdom and has freed himself for further exploration of the "spirit of the continent" (Crane's alternate title for "Cape Hatteras") in the second half of *The Bridge*. The circle of the dance gives way to the straight line of "other calendars" that "now stack the sky," the skyscrapers of twentieth century Manhattan. But he has learned from the Indians the possibilities of the body and the natural passions, and he affirms that Maquokeeta gazes through "infinite seasons" at his "bride immortal in the maize" (with perhaps a pun on "maze"). He has experienced the power of love to liberate, the truth of the "Sabbatical" smile, as Pocahontas has liberated Maquokeeta: "Thy freedom is her largessee, Prince, and hid/ On paths thou knewest best to claim her by." He recognizes that Pocahontas, Eros, is still "the torrent and the singing tree;/ And she is virgin to the last of men..." Her "speechless dream of snow" is set to "singing" by the sun in a seasonal cycle which is never-ending, and the imagery of speech and song associates this cycle with the creative process leading to poetry itself. Pocahontas is a sort of Muse, and a symbol of Eros, urging the unitive imagination to further creation of its life in forms. Her association in the imagination's life with "bloom" and love in the present is suggested. The water-cycle continues, the dream of "snow" becoming "winds" and finally a "stream," and the circle of the poet's journey is completed by the return "West, west and south."

The poem concludes with the poet's new questions, cast in the present tense, as to the endurance of the truth of

Indian civilization: "And when the caribou slant down for salt/ Do arrows thirst and leap? Do antlers shine/ Alert, star-triggered in the listening vault/ Of dusk?—And are her perfect brows to thine?" The questions really concern the efficacy of the dance, the act of imagination, in saving from time the Indian civilization. The answer is ambiguous: "We danced, O Brave, we danced beyond their farms,/ In cobalt desert closures made our vows....Now is the strong prayer folded in thine arms,/ The serpent with the eagle in the boughs." The only thing affirmed is the dance, and that in the past tense. But the poet identifies with Maquokeeta, acknowledges his participation in the dance, and affirms that the "strong prayer," which in the beginning of "The Dance" brought water to the "mesa sands," is no longer "forgotten" but "folded in thine arms," the bride "immortal" in the organic "maize" of the Indian's natural world.

5. Indiana

The beginning of "Indiana" is accompanied by a margin gloss ("...and read her in a mother's farewell gaze") that connects this section with the rest of "Powhatan's Daughter." The gloss ends the sentence begun at the opening of "The Dance" ("Then you shall see her truly....."), with the important shifts from "her" to "mother" and "see" to "read." The lower-Pocahontas has here become a mother, both the pioneer mother who sings the song and the Indian squaw met on "the long trail back" from chasing false gods, fool's gold, in Colorado. Both women are widows bearing fatherless sons, the remnants of their marriages. And the pioneer woman's assumption of the Indians' nature-symbolism comes from "reading," from reflection rather than re-enactment of the physical union of "The Dance," from a mediated mode of transmission. Similarly, the poet is dumb in this section, suggesting that the body's attempt to communicate its truth through biological generation is a silent process. It can be known only through reflection, as we must "read" in a "farewell gaze" the implicit record of the sound and fury that accompanied the creative act itself, the "bison thunder" that, as the pioneer woman says, "rends my dreams no more/ As once my womb was torn, my boy, when you/ Yielded your first cry at the prairie's door...."

In spite of the fact that "Indiana" is a monologue, the piece is characterized by pregnant silences: that of "all our silent men," of the squaw who "Knew that mere words could not have brought us nearer," and of Larry himself, who never interrupts or responds to his mother's words. "Indiana" begins with an image of silence, and a suggestion of coming death: "The morning glory, climbing the morning long/ Over the lintel on its wiry vine,/ Closes before the dusk, furls in its song/ As I close mine...." The closing circles of the morning glory flower, the mouth of the singer and, in the second stanza, the womb of the pioneer woman, all suggest the cessation of creative activity. This is affirmed by the pioneer woman later when she exclaims, "I'm standing still, I'm old, I'm half of stone!" The "bloom" which concluded "The Dance" has here disappeared, and all that's left is the record of bloom and fruitfulness, which Larry and the reader both are instructed to "read" in the mother's "farewell gaze," to glean from her record of her experiences of hunting for gold and God. The "morning glory" is fading, and its only hope of survival is in Larry, in his "eyes' engaging blue," the cosmic, oceanic azure where her whispers play. The pioneer mother has learned that continuing life, generation and birth, is truer than gold. And she acknowledges that in her son's eyes is "Where gold is true."

That the end and purpose of the body's truth is a further affirmation of life and motion is suggested in "Indiana" by the contrast between generation, the "true gold," and materialism, the false God. The pioneer woman recalls her trip with Jim, her dead husband, to the gold fields of Colorado, where gold was "God." The theme of materialism, present but understated throughout *The Bridge*, here becomes dominant: the values of materialism are a threat to the continuing life of the imagination. "A dream called Eldorado was his town,/ It rose up shambling in the nuggets' wake,/ It had no charter but a promised crown/ Of claims to stake."[12]

The threat of materialism to the life of the imagination is emphasized by the puns on "gold" and "God" in this section, and the particular threat is that of the static to the dynamic, of the dead and barren to the living and fruitful. It is appropriate, and significant, that materialism should be emphasized here as a threat to generation, for "Indiana" follows the successful assimilation and integration of the body of the continent by the imagination. In Crane's poetics the step following the successful assimilation and integration of experience into the living imagination is the process of giving birth to the imagination's new truth in a poem or artifact, which will then bear this living truth onward into the reader's consciousness. Generation is threatened by materialism, as life and growth are threatened by excessive desire for permanence and stasis. The pioneer's search for gold "Won nothing....But gilded promise, yielded to us never,/ And barren tears." The imagery of fruition, or lack thereof, aptly renders the contrast between gold and her son's "true gold," located in his eyes.

The symbolism of the "eyes" in "Indiana" is important. They are the bearers and conveyers of vision, and are opposed to the silence of material generation isolated from vision. The "silent men—the long team line" that watches the Indian squaw pass by is shunned by her in favor of the pioneer mother; and the "twin stars" of the squaw's eyes are "Lit with love shine" at the sight of the mother and child.

The twin stars recall the "winter king" and the "glacier woman" of "The Dance," and suggests that the truth of the Dance resides in the squaw's eyes, and from them is passed to the pioneer mother, as the wisdom of the body endures in the Female. Similarly, the eyes of Larry are the circles which encompass the unitive truth of the pioneer mother's life, the beginning and the end of her "stubborn" and "still-born" years: "I'm standing still, I'm old, I'm half of stone!/ Oh, hold me in those eyes' engaging blue;/ There's where the stubborn years gleam and atone,—/ Where gold is true!" The contrast by rhyme of "stone" and "atone" subtly points up the conflict of the inert and static materialism with the living and dynamic generation and regeneration. The use of "atone" suggests that Larry is, in terms of biological generation, the son who can reconcile the dead father with the living mother. He is a natural bridge, for he has his father's eyes ("And you're the only one with eyes like him"), and his mother measures her life by the memory of her dead husband Jim ("As long as Jim, your father's memory, is warm"). He is the descendant of pioneers, the natural vehicle for the continuation of the search for "God."

But the Indians' experience of the unity of nature, imparted from the squaw to the mother of Larry, does not survive. The sailor's eyes in "Cutty Sark" have undergone a sea-change, and he keeps "weakeyed watches." The body's powers, so gloriously displayed in "The Dance," give way in "Indiana" to a rendering of the body's inherent limitations. The body has a fundamental role in the organic life of the imagination, providing the source of energy, the erotic "pure impulse inbred" ("Cape Hatteras") that motivates the imagination's life. The impulse to creation and generation, the truth of the "body of the continent" and the imagination's dependence on the body, is the essential beginning of spiritual articulations, as the natural flight of the gull in "Proem" urged the poet toward the Bridge. But mere physical generation is not enough to create an organic construct capable of enduring and embodying the truth of the imagination, as witness "Indiana" and "Cutty Sark." Hence the imagination turns to other poets in the second half of *The Bridge* for instruction in the spirit of the continent and the articulation of that spirit, moving always toward a fusion of body and spirit in the Bridge itself.

CHAPTER 6

Cutty Sark

"Cutty Sark" concludes the first half of *The Bridge*, according to Crane's own division of the poem; it completes the imagination's circular journey in terms of the body through time and memory to mythic Everpresence, then back to the quotidian world, which began in "The Harbor Dawn." The time of "The Harbor Dawn" has given way here to the dawn of another day, as the poet finds himself crossing over the Bridge to his apartment, the "home" where he first glimpsed Pocahontas in a "waking dream," "Cutty Sark" divides into two parts, the first rendering the nocturnal meeting of the poet and the derelict sailor in a bar, the second the poet's projected vision from his place on the Bridge of the glorious days of the clipper ships. The subject of the first part is the failure of the derelict sailor, a metamorphosis of the ranging Larry of "Indiana," to keep the faith of his mother in the "true gold" of the unitive act of loving generation. The subject of the second part is the poet's vision of the success of "clipper dreams indelible and ranging" in tracing the symbolic circle as they circumnavigate the globe, realizing their unitive urge. They "Heave, weave/ those bright designs the trade winds drive," with "Bright skysails ticketing the Line" as they "wink around the Horn/ to Frisco, Melbourne..." This vision inspires the poet, counteracting the failure of the derelict sailor, and urges him onward toward the realization of his own dream of act.

The epigraph of "Cutty Sark" suggests the iron dealt cleavage in terms of the sea and sailing: "O, the navies old and oaken,/ O, the Temeraire no more!" (Melville). The derelict sailor of this section was "A whaler once," but now he's separated from those "oaken" navies and hired out to the iron-clads, caught up in the materialism that has separated modern America from the spiritual and mythic legacies of "The Dance." The generative possibilities of the organic, suggested in "oaken," have given way to the sterility of iron, and images of sterility cluster around the sailor. He is wife-less, like the hoboes of the River, and the admission that the "damned white Arctic killed my time" suggests his loss of sexual as well as imaginative powers. Further, his association with the "donkey engine," a forerunner of the Faustian "cavalcade on escapade" of "Cape Hatteras," emphasizes the sterile nature of his allegiance to the iron machine. The "engaging" blue eyes of Larry have undergone a sea-change, for the sailor's eyes are "GREEN," his "eyes pressed through green glass/ —green glasses, or bar lights made them/ so—/ shine—/ GREEN—/ eyes—. The color of hope and growth is ironically applied to this sterile denizen of South Street. He can't break the confining repetitions of the "donkey engine" to build "some white machine that sings," can't free his imagination to raised "ATLANTIS ROSE" and Love itself.

The identification of the sailor with the "voice of Time" is obvious in his speech: "I'm not much good at time any more keep/ weak-eyed watches sometimes snooze—" his bony hands/ got to beating time./ ..."A whaler once—/ I ought to keep time and get over it—I'm a/ Democrat—I know what time it is—No/ I don't want to know what time it

is—that/ damned white Arctic killed my time…" Even such
a subtle distinction between the voices of Eternity (the "Atlantis" theme) and the sailor's being a "Democrat," rather
than a Platonic Republican, points up his identification with
the world of time. The sailor is caught in a world of bar hours
and sailing deadlines, his time and vision killed by the Arctic,
that land inhabited by the "glacier woman," Pocahontas,
who is available only to those who know how to claim her.
Rather than being entertained by Pocahontas, the "singing
tree" of "The Dance," the sailor's voice is contrapuntal with
the juke box's song of "O Stamboul Rose," who is transmuted into "ATLANTIS ROSE" and the voice of eternity.
The "voice of Eternity," rendered in italics, describes a general, eternally recurring process of which the sailor is a particular example, thus providing the basal motif of the fugue.
The verbal shift from the initial "O Stamboul Rose—dreams
weave the rose" through "O Stamboul Rose—drums weave—"
and "green—drums—drown—" to the final "ATLANTIS
ROSE drums wreathe the rose" is a shift (from "dreams"
to "drums" and "weave" to "wreathe") which suggests the
purgation the poet must undergo if he is to carry the truth
of the first half of *The Bridge* through to "Atlantis." It is a
purgation which has "killed" the vision and time of the
sailor. A descent to Atlantis must precede the raising of that
condemned island, here associated with Pompeii and Vesuvi-
us via the imagery of "water-gutted lava" and the creative
imagination in general; and the image of the "star" that
floats burning in a gulf of tears prepares for the image of the
poet triumphantly floating on the "Anemone," whose
"petals spend the suns about us," in "Atlantis." The contrast
reflects the difference between the stages of suffering and
resurrection in the three-fold process of the imagination, between the death through assimilation and the subsequent
liberation and individuation.

The poet is the one whose imagination transmutes the song
on the jukebox into the voice of eternity, rather than the

sailor, who remains impervious and unimaginative throughout. It is the poet who perceives the possibilities of the imagination, even in the unredeemed bedlamite sailor: "I saw the frontiers gleaming of his mind;/ or are there frontiers—running sands sometimes/ running sands—somewhere—sands running/.../ Or they may start some white machine that sings./ Then you may laugh and dance the axletree—/ steel-silver—kick the traces—and know—" The "white machine" is the imagination, which in the sailor is frozen. It is imagistically associated with the jukebox that is "weaving somebody's nickel," and whose song the poet himself is weaving to his imagination's purposes. The image of dancing "the axletree' recalls the Dance as well as the progression from "series on series, infinite" to the unitive vision of the "turning rondure whole" in "Ave Maria." It suggests the sailor's potential liberation from the linear wagon "traces," and his succession to the circle of "steel-silver," the turning "axletree," where he might "know...ATLANTIS ROSE...interminably," realizing in time the truth and "Everpresence" of his imagination's power. But the sailor does not proceed this way; instead, he leaves the bar, moving on up "Bowery way." The first half of "Cutty Sark" ends with the poet leaving the "cooler hells" of the bar, and the imprisoned and loveless sailor, as "the dawn/ was putting the Statue of LIberty out—that/ torch of hers you know—."

The concluding half of "Cutty Sark" presents the poet's vision of the clipper ships from the Bridge. The fact that the poet is on the Bridge is not especially emphasized, since at this stage of the imagination's life the Bridge is yet to be perceived as the symbolic "Bridge to Thee, O Love." Still, the Bridge is here the construction from which the poet can project a fantasy out of that past through which he has just journeyed, as he reminds us of his role as *homo faber*, the maker, and of his act, the structuring of words.

The metaphor of weaving renders both the motion of the ships over the oceans and, more subtly, the arrangement of

the words on the page of the poem itself. The images of ships
as "vanities" and "repartees" suggest their identification with
their word-names on the page; and the force that motivates
both ships and word-names to "weave/ those bright designs"
is that of the "trade winds" ("the vibrant breath" of "Sibyl-
line voices" in "Atlantis"), symbol of the shaping imagination. The designs themselves are both the flags the ships carry
and the patterns of their motions across the surface of the
sea: "Pennants, parabolas—/ clipper dreams indelible and
ranging,/ baronial white on lucky blue!" And the design of
"parabolas" recalls that earlier image of the life of man, the
"parable of man," which associated the life of the imagination and the curve it traces with the curve of the Bridge itself. Here the curves of the ships on the sea's surface are a
series of Bridge-like parabolas, associating their voyaging
efforts with the poet's own journey toward the Bridge, the
"Tall Vision-of-the-Voyage" of "Atlantis," and by extension
contrasting the poet with the derelict sailor of the first half
of "Cutty Sark." The poet's ability to project this fantasy of
"clipper dreams" suggests that he has successfully overcome
the obstacles which defeated the vision of the derelict sailor.
The "tragedy" of the sailor's failure to "start some white
machine that sings" has, for the moment at least, been
avoided by the poet. He has assimilated what in "Cape Hatteras" he refers to as "all that time has really pledged us,"
and is ready to confront "Space, instantaneous" in the
second half of *The Bridge*, to wake from dreams of the past
into the dream of act. "Cutty Sark" (and the first half of *The
Bridge*) ends on a questioning invocation of the lost ship
"Ariel," whose name suggests the creative spirit of *The Tempest*, the power which may empower the poet to "wrap harness to the swarming air" in the exploration of space to
come.

PART III
The Spirit of the Continent

CHAPTER 7

Cape Hatteras

"Cape Hatteras" is introduced by an epigraph which not only invokes Whitman but also indicates that the journey of the first half of *The Bridge* has been completed: "The seas all crossed,/ weathered the capes, the voyage done." The initial images of the poem suggest some of the ramifications of this major conclusion-beginning in *The Bridge*. The opening lines continue the use of visual typographical arrangement which marked the conclusion of "Cutty Sark," thus providing a sense of continuity even within the dynamic change which the images themselves render. The descent-ascent motion is visually represented, especially in the descending lines. The image of the "dinosaur...the mammoth saurian/ ghoul," recalls the "serpent" of time, here dropping out of sight. The "eagle" of space in this second half of the poem "dominates our days," replacing time as the most important coordinate of the imaginative act, the spanning Bridge. The descent into the past and the body of the continent, which provided the subject of the first half of *The Bridge*, is here replaced by ascent into the present and the realm of the spirit and space, as the imagination prepares for the act that will create the

Bridge. The source of energy is still "Combustion at the astral core," the "Fire" which in "Ave Maria" symbolized the creative power of the Word. But the direction of the energy has shifted upwards in a "dorsal change." Both the spiritual analogue and the upward redirection of the imagination's "pure" impulse are rendered in the etymological ambiguities of "dorsal." The word suggests not only the dorsal fin of the fish (Crane's marine counterpart of the horse—both symbols of unadulterated natural energy) but also the "dorsal" of an altar, the place where the focus of the congregation is architecturally redirected from the minister upwards toward heaven. The "convulsive," "Imponderable" nature of this shift of primal energies at the heart, the "astral core" of the planet itself, the center of the earth, demands the recognition of a fundamental change in the momentum of the imagination.

The "dorsal change of energy" is paralleled by the poet's return "home to our own/ Hearths" (unindividuated at this beginning, he uses the editorial "we"), a more human shift, as suggested in the subtle contrast between cosmic combustion and the homey fires of "hearths" (with, perhaps, a pun on human "hearts"). The rounding of the world by the clipper ships of "Cutty Sark" is here completed: the result is the knowledge that "strange tongues" of other lands and cultures merely "vary messages of surf/ Below grey citadels, repeating to the stars/ The ancient names." The emphasis is on "vary," for the exploration of the physical body of the continent, or of the world via "clipper dreams," has taught the poet that nature's "messages of surf," and the "pure impulse inbred" of the imagination's unitive urge, are not different but only varied by "strange tongues." The poet suggests that the return to specifically American variations of "messages of surf" will be a return "to read you, Walt," to Whitman's poetic record of the message of the "wraith/ Through surf, its bird note there a long time falling," and of the coexistence of "living brotherhood" and love with this "wraith." The circling of the world in "clipper dreams" gives way to the circle of the poet's unitive eye that encompasses the seeming opposites of war and love, destruction and creation, within its "primal scan."

Before proceeding to the airplane and Whitman's poetry, which are the two new subjects introduced in this section, the poet presents an imagistic resume recalling Whitman's "Passage to India" as well as the first half of *The Bridge*. Its subject is the myths of the past which the imagination must bring into the present in order that it can give song to what Whitman called the "voiceless earth" (here the "hushed land") and project itself into the future. The movement through the American past has been similar to that in the first half of Whitman's "voyage" of the "Mind's return./ To reason's early paradise,/ Back, back to wisdom's birth, to innocent intuitions,/ Again with fair creation." The poet is "in thrall/ To that deep wonderment, our native clay," to Pocahontas and the wisdom of the body, the "depth of red, eternal flesh of Pocahontas." Her flesh, and his own body are "veined by all that time has really pledged us," repositories of what he later terms the "pure impulse inbred." The imagery of the "sweetness" of the "continental folded aeons" lying "below derricks, chimneys, tunnels" continues the physical and sexual imagery which links poetic creation with generation itself. Further, the masculine is associated with machinery, just as the Female is the fertile land. The union suggested by the penetration of "derricks, chimneys, tunnels" into the land is of the mechanical and pastoral, a union necessary to the creation of the organic construct of the Bridge in "Atlantis," where the "cities are endowed/ And justified conclamant with ripe fields." Above these pledges of time sits the "world of wires and whistles" glimpsed briefly in "The River"; and "thin squeaks of radio static,/ The captured fume of space foams in our ears." The first half of

The Bridge is recalled in the "whisperings of far watches on the main" heard in "Cutty Sark" and "Ave Maria." They are now "Relapsing into silence, while time clears/ Our lenses, lifts a focus, resurrects/ A periscope to glimpse what joys or pain/ Our eyes can share or answer," a prelude to the imagination's recognition of its new "dream of act." Of key significance in this imagery of vision is the "periscope," which etymologically suggests "vision around," the encompassing vision of the symbolic circle. This inclusive scope is symbolic of the unitive act, which frees both poet and poem from that labyrinth "where each sees only his dim past reversed." Mimesis is discarded in favor of inspiration (as Whitman is "joyous seer" and inspiration is a "white seizure" in "Atlantis") in the imagination's dream of embodying its life in a structure, a "breed of towers" and a Bridge. The mirror gives way to the "periscope" which expands and extends rather than blocks and blinds the circle of the poet's eye. Further, the "periscope," in its common association with submarines, reminds us that the poetic vision is generated out of the core, the "depth of red" which is the pure energy of life itself, the motive of the organic imagination.

The third stanza of "Cape Hatteras" opens with an affirmation that in spite of the deflection of vision the imagination's unitive impulse still abides in the poet's periscopic eye (what Whitman in "Eidolons" called the poet's "orbic tendencies to shape and shape and shape" the symbolic circles, eidolons, of the unitive vision). The circle here is the round aperture of the periscope and the eye as well as the spatial circle of the horizon: it is the cipher of unity, what Emerson in "Circles" called the primary figure of the world. The Christian analogue of the imagination's act is subtly continued in "salver," especially in its conjunction with "crucible," which associates the circle with the round plate held under the mouth of the religious communicant to keep the host from falling to the ground. The word's derivation from the Latin "salvare" ("to save") suggests the redemptive aspects of the unitive act symbolized by the circle, which the adjective "blind" directly connects with sight and the eye-vision-imagination motif. Though "sluiced by motion" the unitive impulse, the circle-crucible-eye is "subjugated never." The poet's insistence later in "Cape Hatteras" that man must not subjugate but "conjugate infinity's dim marge—/ Anew" emphasizes the organic, conjugal relationship between the circle and the elements it encloses, between the creator and the creation of his primal scan.

The stanza continues the vision imagery, expanding the scope of the deflection of vision to the "labyrinth submersed" by associating the Fall of Man with the failure of the mimetic ideal: how can a mirror-reflection of a fallen world give an image of man's interior "truth" and worth that is not solipsistic? "Adam and Adam's answer in the forest/ Left Hesperus mirrored in the lucid pool." The fall from grace begat a condition of disunion, the separation of man from God, leaving Hesperus (Venus) forever "mirrored" rather than united in love with man and earth. In "Cape Hatteras" the search for an external God via the airplane fails (the search extensionally through "endless space"). The source of salvation, of spiritual articulations, is located within man, in the "pure impulse inbred" of the imagination. Thus the mimetic dream of reuniting man with God through subjugation and imitation is dismissed by the poet "in this new realm of fact," for the imagination is waking into its "dream of act," a belief in and commitment to the existential power and self-sufficiency of man alone. The mirror-vision in which "each sees only his dim past reversed" must give way to unitive vision "undenying, bright with myth," and inspiration. However, the dimension in which the poet now seeks to establish his "God" is space, the dimension of construction, architecture, vision. Space and time are continuous, as suggested in the phrase "Space, instantaneous." In

terms of the poem, too, space is continuous with time, as
The Bridge, an artifact in space, is also a process unfolding
in time. In this way poetry, an art of time, is also architecture, an art of space, as *The Bridge* is a history of its own
creation. But space, in which the Bridge to Love must be constructed, is here "ambiguous," threatening to transform the
symbolic "smile," the promise of love shared, into a gaping
mouth ("scuttle yawn" in "The Tunnel") which "consumes
us," as much a gulf as that in which time's River died. It is
this gulf of space which the Bridge must structure and span,
and for aid the poet turns to Whitman and his "undenying"
vision, "bright with myth."

Whitman is invoked for his "syllables of faith," his stated
belief that "Recorders ages hence" will find the same "infinity" that he had. Whitman's faith, significantly, is not only
in the absolute of the imagination's truth, but also in the enduring ability of the poet to record that truth, to get down
the "multitudinous Verb" on paper, to "put the serpent with
the eagle in the leaves" of the poem. The poet identifies
himself with Whitman in their common attempt to create an
empire of the imagination, "our" empire, and hints at the
journey to come before Atlantis is raised. He must go
through the city of "canyoned traffic" in "The Tunnel,"
and "Across the hills where second timber strays," where
older empires and dreams have fallen into wilderness on
"Quaker Hill." To liberate the "eyes" of Whitman is to liberate them within the poet's creative act, as Whitman urged
his readers to liberate him within his poetry, to acknowledge
that he himself was there with them. And the image of the
eyes "undenying" links Whitman with that other poetic
ancestor, Poe, who in "The Tunnel" is asked if he "denied"
the "ticket," denied the necessary union of death and creation in the life of the organic imagination.

The imagination's history continues with a description of
the invention of the airplane and its use as a vehicle of des-

truction rather than creation. This long description, fraught with imagistic inversions of the liberating act of creation, serves as contrast to the poetic flight of Walt Whitman, the subject of the third and final section of "Cape Hatteras." The Cape is the locale of both the destruction of the airplane and the raising of the "rainbow's arch," signal of the reclamation of Whitman's "heritage." It suggests the unitive relationship of the seeming contradictories of destruction-creation in the processes of the dialectical imagination, doing so by allusion to the "ghoul-mound," Golgotha, of Christian tradition: the hill of Calvary. The destruction of and by the airplane is integral in this section with the conquest of space, with the building of the Bridge, fused in Whitman's "heritage" of the unity of destruction-creation, machine-pastoral, war and love. Thus the imagination's final affirmation that it has reclaimed that "heritage" suggests that it has liberated itself from the threat posed by the misuse of power symbolized in the airplane for further progress toward the realization of its "dream of act" in the creation of the Bridge.

The airplane is described in images that parody (convert downwards) the imagination's unitive and creative act. Animal imagery abounds: "Behold the dragon's covey"; "War's fiery kennel masked in downy offings"; "Convoy planes, moonferrets"; "scouting griffins." This animal imagery suggests the dehumanization of the process whereby the airplane is made an instrument of war and separation rather than love and union. The animal imagery clashes grotesquely with imagery of medieval chivalric glory (here used ironically, of course) that renders the "tournament of space," the "cavalcade" ("on escapade," a further ironic reduction) with "escutcheoned wings" that falls from the sky, crashing into a "shapeless debris" of "high bravery." This Open Road leads not to love but war: "The soul, by naptha fledged into new reaches/ Already knows the closer clasp of Mars." The traditional chivalric conflict of Mars and Venus (Chaucer's

"Knight's Tale" comes to mind as example) suggests the earlier images of union (the Prince and Pocahontas in "The Dance") and disunion (the wifeless or runaway hoboes of "The River," the sailor of "Cutty Sark"). War is "dispersion," love is union, and union results in further love according to the laws of the imagination. The central symbol of unitive act, the circle, is also parodied here, for the plane spirals downward and in its flight spins "What ciphers risen from prophetic script,/ What marathons new-set between the stars!" Here "prophetic script" is at once contrasted and compared to the earlier "Power's script," for the "ciphers" (circles) offer simultaneously promise and perversion of promise—all and nothing—as suggested in the ambiguous meaning of the word "cipher." In the "tournament of space" the "threshed and chiselled height/ Is baited by marauding circles," of destruction. And at the height of the airplane's dogfighting flight the poet raises the exclamation-question of the truth of a vision that can unify war and love, and raises it in terms of the eye's ability to encompass in its periscopic vision the destructive squadron of the fleet of airplanes: "Surely no eye that Sunward Escadrille can cover!" Again the etymological device is used, for "Escadrille" ultimately derives from "squarare" ("to square"), so that the circle of the eye (symbolic of the unitive vision) is being set against a seemingly intractable square, a form antithetical to the "parable" of man and its geometric counterpart, the parabola of the Bridge.

The description of the airplane's flight concludes in an imagistic and visual rendering of its "down whizzing" path to "mashed and shapeless debris," the reversal of the artfully shaped cartogram of the sea-ships at the end of "Cutty Sark." Rather than a spanning bridge, the machine is "bunched" and "beached" wreckage, as form and shape are dispersed in "gravitation's vortex," the destructive reverse of the unitive act. The poet's directive to the "Falcon-Ace" who pilots the airplane, whose vision and eyes have become "bicarbonated white by speed," is not followed here, but stands as indication of the path that must be taken if the imagination is to realize its dream of act; "Remember, Falcon-Ace,/ Thou hast there in thy wrist a Sanskrit charge/ To conjugate infinity's dim marge—/ Anew...! Union rather than domination is the "Sanskrit charge," the original directive, the "pure impulse imbred," which must be the standard for the utilization of the machine for human freedom. The warning of this "Sanskrit charge" to "conjugate" rather than "subjugate" infinity is clear, and the image continues the association of the primal force of the imagination and the recording of that primal act in language; thus it prepares for the final invocation of Whitman, with his "New integers of Roman, Viking, Celt," as the poetic master whose records of the word redeem the destruction of war and of the body in war by turning that destruction to imaginative creation. Following the asterisk comes a long and even paean which stands in glaring contrast to the near-grotesque gyrations of language in the rendering of the descent of the airplane. To the knowledge of the body is here added the loving force of poetry, as "The competent loam, the probable grass" are linked with the "rebound seed" of Whitman's poetry. Religious imagery, associating the efficacious influence of Whitman's "heritage" with the Resurrection, contrasts with the animal imagery (and imagery of the empty chivalric ideal) to suggest the redemptive relationship of poetry to the Faustian spirit; Whitman's records of "Junctions elegiac, there, of speed/ With vast eternity" become "Easters of speeding light" when rendered in poetry, as the imagination affirms itself in its creation. And "upward from the dead" Whitman resurrects a "new bound," "rebound" pact, vibrant unitive vision of "living brotherhood." His efforts are generated out of the "pure impulse inbred" that links the unitive creative impulse, the imagination, with the laws of nature, "loam/ ...grass...tides." Whitman's response

to the "old persuasions" of the "stars," the "theme that's
statured on the cliff," has generated a poem, "a pact new
bound/ of living brotherhood" that embodies the imagination's rebinding of "The stars" and "deepest soundings."

The symbolic function of Whitman's poetic constructions
uniting the furthest reaches of space and the "deepest soundings," the "pure impulse inbred," is emphasized in the next
stanza, where Whitman is a bridge spanning "beyond/ Glacial
sierras and the flight of ravens" to "this, thine other hand,
upon my heart." For the poet Whitman is the bridge uniting
in "The Open Road" suffering with exaltation, descent with
ascent. Whitman is the poet who "Hast kept of wounds, O
Mourner, all that sum/ That then from Appomattox stretched
to Somme!", the poet of suffering as well as healing. And it
is this "truth" of Whitman's poems which the poet of *The
Bridge* integrates into the living imagination, in the same way
that he integrated the unitive myth of the Indian culture by
identifying with Maquokeeta and participating in the Dance.
The next stanza simultaneously describes the poet's first
reading of Whitman and parallels that experience with earlier
parts of *The Bridge*. Whitman's poetry is identified with nature itself, with land and sea in their common impulse toward
fruition and renewal. The reading of the poetry is identified
with a reliving of that poetry, a searching of "the hill/ Blue-
writ and odor-firm with violets." The poet remembers that
"White banks of moonlight" (like "white buildings") were
"How speechful," as he responded to them "vibrantly,"
hearing "thunder's eloquence" and "trumpets breathing."
His movement through the organic world of Whitman's poetry continued until "Gold autumn, captured, crowned the
trembling hill!" This image renders the achievement of the
unitive act, here for Whitman's poetic construct in terms of
the circle of the unitive vision, the "crown" (recalling the
"kindled crown" of "Ave Maria"), with the added implication of organic fruition as concomitant with the organic

imagination and its organic construct. Perhaps the most important addition here is the association of speech and writing with the unitive act (recall that Maquokeeta was dumb), for it suggests that the new stage of the imagination involves its recognition of the necessity of embodying its truth in poetry, in a record which can live beyond the death of the poet himself. Whitman has not only achieved a unitive truth of death and resurrection, he has left a record which lives "beyond."

The next stanza renders the significance of Whitman for the poet in terms of the Bridge. Whitman is *"Panis Angelicus!"* He is the angelic bread, food for the imagination (and contrasted with the machine that leaves men "hungry on the tracks"); his eyes are "tranquil with the blaze/ Or love's own diametric gaze, of love's amaze!" The image of "love's amaze," via a pun on "maize" and "maze," renders the organic resurrection (verbally, at least) of the "labyrinth" (sunken Atlantis) by the force of love, locating the "empire" of the imagination in the poems of Whitman (although that "empire" has not yet been founded in the confining "world of stocks," Manhattan). The symbolic circle of the unitive vision is suggested in the image of "diametric gaze," and the paradox of "tranquil with the blaze" renders the unity of opposites which characterizes the symbolic circle. Whitman's poetry is for the poet "onward yielding past my utmost year," a living thing that lives with the poet, and is organic ("yielding") as the poet himself is organic. Whitman is "Familiar," yet "Evasive—too—as dayspring's spreading arc to trace is," a sort of organic element residing in organic nature, as much liberated in the elements of his cosmos—his poetic world—as Maquokeeta was in the elements of his nature-myth. Whitman's connection with the Bridge is definite: "Our Meistersinger, thou set breath in steel;/ And it was thou who on the boldest heel/ Stood up and flung the span on even wing/ Of that great Bridge, our Myth, whereof I sing!" This is the "Myth" proper to Whitman and the poet, rather

than the nature-myth of Maquokeeta; it is the myth of the
imagination's power to assimilate and use the fact of the machine to build a Bridge "to Thee, O Love." It recalls Whitman's use of the boat in "Crossing Brooklyn Ferry," or his
poem "To a Locomotive in Winter." The image of the "boldest heel" associates Whitman with Elohim and the "sounding
heel" of "Ave Maria," suggesting the association of poetic
creation and cosmic creation, and the inclusion of the Bridge
in that same breath defines the goal of the poet himself: the
creation of a world through an architecture of words, the setting of "breath in steel," the Bridge, as the Logos set breath
in human clay itself.

The ability of Whitman to move through death to a new
life in his poems is the subject of the next stanza. The "Barrier" is known "leastwise" (both "at least" and in the un-
wisest fashion) as "death-strife" (death and war and destruction), and Whitman has "passed" death by incorporating himself (and "us") in "something green," a poem "throbbing"
(the imagination's organic propulsion) "with one voice."
The organic imagination spans beyond the logic of "science,"
the hocus-pocus of scientific "sesames," and discovers "New
integers," which unify in a "pact, new-bound" the "living
brotherhood." In "greensward" is a pun on "green word,"
the living word, the organic "Multitudinous Verb" (Verb,
rather than noun, to suggest action) of the poem itself. Whitman made a "choice," a conscious selection of alternatives,
kneeling to "something green," the "greensward," life itself
as well as the living imagination. He made this "choice"
which the poet of *The Bridge* makes in this and the sections
following, as he is henceforth empowered by Whitman's example.

This acknowledgment of Whitman's "heritage" empowers
the poet to perceive space as a circle made up of "abysmal
cupolas," depths and heights simultaneously. Whitman's
poems, paradoxes of man's "parable," are "endless terminals,

Easters of speeding light" toward which the poet's imagination, a resurrected airplane, moves "with seraphic grace/ On clarion cylinders pass out of sight." The imagination has assimilated and disarmed the Faustian spirit embodied in the airplane, liberating itself to "course that span of consciousness," the "history" of the Bridge itself; and Whitman's "vision is reclaimed!/ What heritage thou'st signalled to our hands!" Here the poet invokes his own "hands," the instruments of creation (as in the "Hand of Fire"), as well as Whitman's, and affirms the "heritage" and the freedom for further movement which it has given him. Concrete language and primal symbols (rainbow and ghoul-mound, veins and pasture-shine) abound in this conclusion, organic imagery that affirms the living legacy of Whitman, heard in the "veins uncancelled," read in the unitive circle of Whitman's poetry. "Recorders ages hence, yes," including the poet of *The Bridge*, shall affirm Whitman's poetry as a "condition of life" demanding "new spiritual articulations," as a record that lives, as a Bridge to further life. And the poet's recognition of his filial relationship with Whitman, and his concomitant recognition of the continuing life of Whitman's choice of "something green," frees him for his own movement "onward without halt" toward his own unitive act in "Atlantis" and the recording of it in *The Bridge*.

CHAPTER 8

Three Songs

In "Three Songs" the imagination explores the possibilities
of appealing to and possessing love in the modern world.
Each song addresses a type of Woman: Eve, Magdalene, or
Mary, who are associated with memory, desire and imagination, as well as with a song, a dance and a building. Thus the
progression is an analogue of the three-step poetic process
delineated by Crane, as well as synecdoche of the process
which engendered *The Bridge* itself. Crane employs the traditional Christian schema of Eve, Magdalene, and Mary only
to pass through it, for the "Cathedral Mary" that is invoked
in "Virginia" and asked to "shine" inhabits a "white building" of the poet's own making. Thus in "Three Songs" the
imagination turns the Romantic expressionistic song against
itself, reveals its inadequacies in this "new realm of fact,"
and then in "Virginia" moves beyond, toward a form more
appropriate to the organic construct of *The Bridge*.

The epigraph to "Three Songs," taken from Marlowe's
Hero and Leander, alludes to an attempt to bridge a strait
to Love. The two cities of the legend, "The one Sestos, the
other Abydos hight," are opposite each other on the Darda-

nelles Straits. In the classical story (and in Marlowe's poem) Leander swam the Hellespont each night to Hero, guiding himself by a light that shone from the tower where Hero attended the swans and sparrows dedicated to Venus. He drowned one night when a tempest arose as he was swimming toward his tower beacon. The parallels between the poet's efforts to unite with Love in "Three Songs" and Leander's nightly swim to Hero's "love light" (recall that phrase from "Indiana") is emphasized by the role of the tower light in each case, for Cathedral Mary is urged to "Shine...Out of the way-up nickel-dime tower shine." The invocation of Leander (in "Cutty Sark" the "last trip" of the ship Leander was a "tragedy") recalls the threat of death involved in each bridging, a concomitant of the search for rebirth and creation through union with love in *The Bridge*.

The first song, "Southern Cross," renders the failure of the poet to discover in a traditional Female type of love, Eve, someone to share "utterly" his urge for love and union in love. The poet wants the "nameless Woman of the South" (Eve, Magdalene, or Mary—he tries all three names in the three Songs) as a mate in marriage, "No wraith, but utterly," but his call "falls vainly on the wave," and Eve becomes a "wraith of my unloved seed." The Song concludes in an imagistic *reductio* of the white buildings hoped for from the union: "Light drowned the lithic trillions of your spawn." The spawn of "lithic trillions" drowned by light, like the flesh rendered "sandstone grey" by the failure of light in the next Song, are stillborn constructions, incapable of supporting life. The imagery of speech ("utterly," "call," "whispering hell," "namelessness") which renders this failure suggests its association with poetry and the fulfillment of the "dream of act" through the creation of poems. The Southern Cross moves upward in the night's sky, removing "girdles" from night as it goes (spiraling upwards, but not "building Liberty"). The Cross and the "nameless Woman" are "high, cool,/

wide from the slowly smoldering fire/ Of lower heavens"
such as that of the National Winter Garden or Manhattan described in the next two Songs. They are too high for the
poet's song to reach, unresponsive "phantoms" of a tradition,
unable to survive the "light" in the modern world's new
realm of fact.

The aspect of love explored in "National Winter Garden"
is the physical, the type of woman invoked is Magdalene, and
the setting is Minsky's, the famous burlesque house in lower
Manhattan. Rather than the high, cool abode of night in the
"Southern Cross," this locale is one of the "lower heavens,—
vaporous scars," a smoke-filled noisome auditorium. The
poet's desire for Eve as "No wraith, but utterly" is ludicrous-
ly burlesqued by the flesh: "Outspoken buttocks in pink
beads/ Invite the necessary cloudy clinch/ Of bandy eyes."
The poet is assaulted by the flesh, repulsed by its similarity
to yet debasement of his ideal of love, but by the end of the
poem he recognizes that he cannot "flee her spasm through a
fleshless door," cannot avoid the flesh, but must come back
to "die alone" in the body if he is to move from the "backward" vision of "Southern Cross" to the "lifeward" vision
that Magdalene and the body offer. His choice for life involves the loss, the "death" of his ideal of escape through re-
pression of the flesh; and for aid in this movement from
death to birth the poet invokes Magdalene, "the burlesque of
our lust—and faith," the Christian whore-with-the-heart-of-
gold who was not only redeemed in the flesh by Christ but
also discovered Him similarly liberated from the "enchained
Sepulchre" of the Tomb, risen *in the flesh*. Thus she knows
the wisdom of the body in a way that neither Eve nor Mary
do, and appropriately invites the "necessary cloudy clinch,"
the physical union "necessary" to the eventual individuation
and liberation of the poet, his rebirth "bone by infant bone"
which will enable him, free him, to "build" a "Cathedral
Mary" in "Virginia."

There are many instances of imagistic burlesque of earlier ideals of love (Pocahontas, the Virgin, Eve) that support the theme of the unity of "our lust—and faith." The name National Winter Garden, and the dance, burlesque the dance that led to "bloom" in "The Dance," as well as "gardenless" Eve; and the music of "A tom-tom scrimmage with a somewhere violin" recalls both "The Dance" and the "windswept guitars" of "Southern Cross," reducing both noble and romantic music to "the lewd trounce of a final muted beat." But if the dancer burlesques "our faith," she also burlesques "our lust," for her attractiveness comes not from the flesh itself, but from the play of lights on her flesh: she is one of the "panoramic sleights" of "Proem," a "flashing scene" that is never "disclosed," that depends for its effect on speed and light, illusion rather than substance: "And shall we call her whiter than the snow?/ Sprayed first with ruby, then with emerald sheen—/ Least tearful and least glad (who knows her smile?)/ A caught slide shows her sandstone grey between." Even lust is an illusion, a light-trick that fails when a "caught slide" cuts off the light source and leaves the dancer "sandstone grey," an unilluminated white building. Light is just as inimical here to the flesh as it was to the ideal of Eve in "Southern Cross," since in both cases it is a light from without rather than from within, which is the loci of light in the imagination's white buildings. This repudiation of the projective light of the poet in favor of the radiant light of the artifact (the Bridge, finally) is another way in which Crane has moved beyond the Romantics; so that the dancer of "National Winter Garden" burlesques the "faith" in the power of the imagination to illuminate Love by showing the failure of "panoramic sleights" of Romantic expressionistic poetry. The symbolic circle of the unitive vision is here burlesqued: "Her eyes exist in swivellings of her teats," recalling the bearings with their "oilrinsed circles of blind ecstasy" from "Cape Hatteras." The serpent image associated with Eve (her "stinging coil") in "Southern Cross" is recalled here, as the dancer's "silly snake rings begin to mount, surmount/ Each other—turquoise fakes on tinselled hands." But the threat that Eve posed in "Southern Cross" is here mitigated in the case of Magdalene, and done, typically, through the etymological argument; the modifying "silly" renders not only the ridiculous aspects of the "snake rings," but also, via the etymology, the "innocent" aspects of the serpent rings, suggesting the value this second Song affirms: the flesh is not only a burlesque of our faith, it is innocent of evil intent, and it can "Lug us back lifeward—bone by infant bone," if we do not flee it through the "fleshless door" of the mind. The "National Winter Garden" concludes on the subtle affirmation that the individuation necessary to imaginative creation, and hence to further life in terms of Crane's poetics, can come only when to the flesh "each comes back to die alone" (a use of "die" suggestive of the Renaissance *double entendre* denoting both death and the act of sexual intercourse, an ambiguity based on the integrative aspects of both acts).

The aspect of love explored in "Virginia" is the responsive and regenerative (hence loving) possibilities of the "organic construct" of the imagination's own making. Crane explained the title by referring to this Song as "virgin in process of being 'built,'"[1] and significantly the type of Woman invoked is "Cathedral Mary," inhabiting a construct of the imagination, something humanly approachable (as opposed to the high, cool heavens of Eve in "Southern Cross"). The Song progresses from plain Mary to Cathedral Mary, as the poet builds up the working girl mentioned in the first stanza, so that he is in effect creating his own new ideal, an ideal of the constructive imagination, rather than attaching himself to something already in the world. Interesting too is the imagery of chance that surrounds this building process: "Gone seven—gone eleven,/ And I'm still waiting you—," and "Crap-shooting gangs" suggest that the poet's Song consciously invokes

Luck, committing the imagination to forms emergent from a necessary chaos, as a necessary ingredient in the building process (recall the "lucky blue" banners of the designing clipper ships). Crane believed that the creative process involved luck, chance, a factor on which sometimes the artist must "simply wait,"[2] as here the poet is waiting for Cathedral Mary to "shine." The life of the imagination is fraught with dangers, as here Mary is threatened by the "boss." "On cornices of daffodils/ The slender violets stray" while "Crapshooting gangs in Bleecker reign." The poet multiplies potential threats by subtly echoing earlier situations: "Peonies with pony manes—/ Forget-me-nots at windowpanes" recall the "Neighing canyons" of "The Dance" and the mother's smile seen through the window in "Van Winkle." Many things are at stake in this attempt to create a construct of the imagination's truth.

Against these threatening elements are set "Saturday Mary" (where "Saturday" is etymologically connected with "Sabbath" and freedom) and the "golden hair" that abides in the "High wheat tower" (recalling the "pendant, seething wheat/ Of knowledge" to which the Bridge is "threshold"). Liberation into a new "attitude of spirit," with a morality threshed, "essentialized from experience directly," are the objects of the imagination's creative efforts, and the objects the poet here invokes, as he prepares to move on toward the Bridge. He wants a Cathedral Mary that will shine out as a beacon to guide his spanning journey, and he realizes that he will have to create her himself. Thus "Three Songs" ends with an invocation to the love necessary to the creative imagination, the modern Muse whose light will come to the poet, not from afar but from the interior of his own constructions, the fulfillment of his dream of act.

CHAPTER 9

Quaker Hill

The dominant symbol of "Quaker Hill" associates death and aloofness. A building overlooking a Quaker graveyard, "old Mizzentop, palatial white/ Hostelry," stands atop Quaker Hill itself as a sort of tombstone marking the death of a dream. It is abandoned, vacant of life, and its windows gleam "like eyes that still uphold some dream" only at "sunset," reflecting the feeble light of the dying sun rather than radiating their own light, as the white buildings of the imagination must do (as Cathedral Mary was implored to "shine" even brighter than the "noon of May"). "Old Mizzentop," with its "dormer/ Portholes" for windows, imagistically invites comparison (and contrast) with the radiant nautical Bridge of "Atlantis," whose "White tempest nets" ring "the humming spars,/ The loft of vision, palladium helm of stars." The construction on Quaker Hill substitutes a "silent, cobwebbed patience" for the "humming spars" of the living Bridge, and symbolizes a stoic attitude toward death and suffering which the imagination must move beyond. The "palatial white/ Hostelry" stands over the dead Quakers in a spatial relationship that recalls the "alabaster chambers" of Emily Dickin-

son's famous poem, housing "the meek members of the res-
urrection/ Untouched by morning, and untouched by noon,"
shrouded in darkness. "Old Mizzentop" similarly houses
death, not life. The abandoned hotel stands in stark contrast
to the legacy of the "Meistersinger" of the myth of the
Bridge, Walt Whitman, whose poems evinced the radiant light
of "Sea eyes and tidal, undenying, bright with myth" in the
"Cape Hatteras" section, for the "stoic height" of the construction atop Quaker Hill shows only "death's stare in slow
survey," a mode of vision neither "bright" nor "undenying."

The movement through "Quaker Hill" from the "death's
stare" of the tower of the abandoned hotel to the affirmation
of the need to "descend as worm's eye to construe/ Our love
of all we touch" is rendered in a style more propositional
(rather than dramatically alive) than any other section of *The
Bridge*, reflecting the intellect's subjugation of passion to reflective thought which here threatens the life of the imagination. The ironic tension and distance between the real and
the ideal is delivered through a suitably restricted form, as
stanzas of alternating end-rimes give way only to the even
more restrictive rimed couplets of the concluding two
stanzas; and the attitude of the poet matches this style. But
"Quaker Hill" is more than a bitter diatribe against modern
materialism, and the ironic distance as well as the propositional style that conveys it, are thematically and formally
destroyed (a destruction for the purposes of eventual recreation) at the conclusion of the section. The poet moves
beyond "the resigned factions of the dead" and the irony
that is their solace in factionalism to a recognition and affirmation of the need to transmute the "silence" of death and
the separation of irony into a unitive expression, a "stilly
note" of poetry that, paradoxically, "Breaks us and saves."
The poet's descent from the "stoic height" of "death's stare"
to a "worm's eye" view of the flesh is imagistically joined
with a renewed participation in the organic cycle of the

seasons, a recognition of the unitive nature of life and death. And the final line of the poem is an affirmation of this need to descend from the "stoic height". From the intellectual heights through the flesh of "worm's eye" the poet has moved to a renewed recognition of the unitive nature of the imagination. This final image not only urges him downward into "The Tunnel" but also subtly returns him to the epigraph of "Quaker Hill," the "maple's loom" that weaves the red "autumnal leaf" and the poem of Emily Dickinson, the product of another kind of loom.

Two epigraphs preface "Quaker Hill," and subtly bear witness to the imagination's desire to live beyond the death in time and space (as with "Old Mizzentop") of old philosophies or dogmas. The first epigraph, taken from the dancer Isadora Duncan, a favorite of Crane's, is the more propositional of the two: "I see only the ideal. But no ideals have ever been fully successful on this earth." This statement does not hold out any immediate suggestion of the possibility of a reconciliation through art of the tension it speaks to, but then Isadora Duncan's medium of creation is not the word but the dance. The second epigraph, however, does: "The gentian weaves her fringes,/ The maple's loom is red.—(Emily Dickinson). The theme of the inseparability of life and death is imaged in terms of nature in this excerpt from a poem Crane knew as "Summer's Obsequies," as purple gentian and blood-red maple weave blossoms that must die. The epigraph prefigures the image from "Atlantis" of "ripe fields/ Revolving through their harvests in sweet torment," and the weaving metaphor is one of those used likewise in *The Bridge* for the poetic process. In Dickinson's ironic poem the speaker's statement that "My departing blossoms/ Obviate parade," and her sardonic "Amen" to the performance of a mock ritual commemorating a death that must signal their own, reveals "Bee and Butterfly" as uncaring for "the seasons fleeting" as the residents of Quaker Hill. But the poet cares, and by her transmutation of silence into song Dickinson creates an organic construct, a poem, that survives her death as well as the death that is its subject. Thus the second epigraph to "Quaker Hill not only establishes the conflict between the ideal and the real, it also bears witness to the resolution of that conflict which the unitive poetic imagination can provide, a resolution in terms of the organic construction of the poem itself.

The first two stanzas of the poem contrast the Quakers' faith in the providential sufficiency of the natural order with the poet's own sophisticated scepticism. The Quakers are free of modern society's materialistic preoccupations, but their passive acceptance of the strife concomitant with change and death is still a threat to the active imagination. The Quakers possess an organic perspective that "never withers," and they keep the "docile edict of the Spring/ That blends March with August Antarctic Skies," an adherence to the organic process-es of the earth. This pastoral abandonment to the inevitabil-ity of "Time's rendings, time's blendings" has its limitations, however, in the view of an imagination which takes its in-spiration from organic *constructions* like the Brooklyn Bridge or white buildings. The Quakers have settled for the pastoral version of "the world dimensional." They do not see *through* the "rich halo" of the Northern Lights that fill "August Ant-arctic skies" (a familiar image from Emily Dickinson) to any-thing beyond; rather, they resemble the hoboes ("The River") "peering in the can," as they perceive "no other thing/ Than grass and snow, and their own inner being." The Quakers' failure to "cast" (both "reflect" and "sow") on the "seasons fleeting" puts them in danger of death by star-vation, a symbolic malnutrition used elsewhere in *The Bridge* to suggest spiritual, i.e., imaginative, deprivation. Thus the Quakers, "awkward, ponderous and uncoy," avoid the "pan-oramic sleights" of a mechanical and materialistic cast of mind only to fall into a "never disclosed" pattern of another sort, the simplistic routine of "cows."

From the "seasons fleeting" which doom the Quakers' Inner Light to the "shifting reprisals" that belie the "store of faith" in the brotherhood of man, the imagination turns to architecture—a building, old Mizzentop, the white edifice that crowns Quaker Hill. The "palatial white/ Hostelry" is one of those "other calendars" that now "stack the sky" ("The Dance"), and it bears witness to the death of the Quaker dream that America might be "the Promised Land," for the "Portholes" and the "central cupola" of the hotel launch only "death's stare in slow survey." But the alternative architecture of the tourist trade, the "new Avalon Hotel" (a remodelling of the "old Meeting House"), though filled with the noisy roar of music "Fresh from the radio," is as doomed by its faith in novelty and constant change as old Mizzentop was by its adherence to "some dream" out of time, and the "New Avalon" does not promise to last any longer than the "gin fizz" that "Bubbles in time to Hollywood's new love-nest pageant."

The recognition of this juxtaposition of failed architectures draws from the poet an ironic declamation of the historical condition. His recognition of the waste land cast of mind that he must find a way through, the intellect's despair at the substitution of material for spiritual values, of the disintegration of the spiritual values themselves and the "patriarch race." "Adams' auction" (a pun on Adam's action) images the imperfect, historical state that threatens the timeless mythic vision; the American dream is sold out to a European type, "Powitzky," and the "woodlouse" eats "the ancient deal/ Table" no matter who owns it. These are the truths of "this new realm of fact," as the old dreams (like the dream still "upheld" by old Mizzentop) are cancelled out. This inescapable recognition of the failure of stoicism's passivity to support the dream of the ideal in the materialistic present causes the poet to repudiate aloofness and detachment. He descends into and transforms in his own living imagination the waste land which his intellectual vision had perceived, discovering in the process an active "patience" that will take him through the Tunnel to the Bridge.

The recognition that the "resigned factions of the dead" preside on Quaker Hill issues into a summary acknowledgement that "the curse of sundered parentage" haunts both the poet and the nation (and, in conjunction with "Adams' auction," the Christian postlapsarian world); it is the curse of separation and antagonism: Indians vs. Yankees, the poet's mother vs. his father, the world's body from the abstracting intellect. These are the dichotomies the unitive imagination must fuse in order to liberate itself for the creative act. The organic perspective of "the hawk's far stemming view," the Quakers' stoic aloofness that "never withers," is incomplete without the "worm's eye" perception that "all we touch" must die, that life is inseparable from death, and that "our love of all we touch" is impermanently housed in the flesh. The poet's descent into the flesh is not a rejection of the intellect in favor of the flesh, but a movement from intellect *through* the flesh to the act of imagination that can unify the two in an affirmation of its own truth, the "one last angelus" of the "throbbing throat" that can transmute the silence of death into life. The descent is followed by the command to "Arise," a call to resurrection and renewal as well as a call to action, to creation; and what is created, "wrung" (and "rung") from "the heart," is a "stilly note/ Of pain," a paradoxical (and, by a pun on "silly" used previously in "National Winter Garden," radically innocent in Blake's sense) song about silence similar to the poem from Emily Dickinson which provides the epigraph. The religious imagery of the "angelus" and the act of communion in taking the "dust," like the Host, "upon your tongue," recalls Crane's substitution of the aesthetic for the religious absolute.

The final transmutation of pain into song which the sound of the whip-poor-will suggests provides the poet with a natural

affirmation of the truth that neither the stoic neglect of life
nor the materialistic attempt to dominate it affords any salvation. The "dim elm-chancels hung with dew" signal the
coming of the dawn (a favorite time for the whip-poor-will's
song), and the "triple-noted clause of moonlight" suggests
not only the three-noted song of the bird (the triadic
"clause" uniting the antinomies of life and death in a rendering of the "parable of man") but also the death of the moon
that, in the unitive cycle of the universe, is complement to
the birth of the sun. The whip-poor-will, then, at once ex-
presses and bridges the "sundered parentage" of moon and
sun, signalling not only a death but also a birth by his song,
so that the "triple-noted clause" urges the poet onward to
further life by its example. The bird's cry, like the "terrific
threshold" of the Bridge ("Proem"), "unhusks" the poet's
heart of "fright," and "yields" (to continue the threshing
imagery) a "patience" that protects "Love from despair,"
enabling it to accept the descent of the autumn leaves in the
hope of eventual regeneration within the world. The "autumnal leaf" subtly returns us to the "maple's loom" and Emily
Dickinson's poem, a muted reminder that the unitive truth
of the living universe finds its ultimate human pattern in the
creative act of the living imagination embodied in the white
buildings of poetry itself. It is toward his own poetic Bridge
that the poet now moves, armed with a patience learned on
Quaker Hill that will aid his passage through the "Gates of
Wrath" of "The Tunnel."

CHAPTER 10
The Tunnel

In "The Tunnel" the imagination, via the poet, submits to the intellect's ironic estimation of modern life, assimilates and moves beyond it, descending through the surface remnants of the past it has already explored to the source *in the present* of the energy which will enable it to create-perceive ("accrete" is the anagram for this dual relationship in "Ave Maria") the Bridge of "Atlantis." The mediate states of dream and memory finally drop away, as it encounters in this section the immediate forces it must fuse to "build Liberty" and realize its dream of act. The journey through the Tunnel is not escape but excavation, the use by the imagination of the now correctly oriented intellect to follow out that "quarrying passion" ("The River") beneath "dead echoes" of the past to its source in itself, the "Word" living still in the present. It is the act of assimilation, the identification with all of life, that in Crane's poetics must precede the construction of white buildings or the building of the Bridge.

The call to "descend—/ descend" that concluded "Quaker Hill" urges the poet via the subway beneath the fragmented surface of Manhattan and the oily waters of the East River, to finally arrive on the Brooklyn side of the Harbor, opposite the "ticking towers" of the Manhattan skyline. The epigraph to "The Tunnel," taken from Blake, links this subway trip with the passage through the "Gates of Wrath" that is necessary for him who seeks "The Western Path" to life's renewal. In Blake's poem it is the Sun itself which is liberated by this journey. The epigraph suggests that the poet's nocturnal subway trip is complement to the diurnal cycle of the Sun and the organic processes of life itself.

The American poet invoked in "The Tunnel" is Edgar Allan Poe. His severed head, suggestive of the death appropriate to the mind's attempt to separate from and dominate the body and imagination, is met in the midst of the journey. The function of Poe is suggested by a letter Crane wrote concerning William Carlos Williams' book, *In The American Grain*: "I was so interested to note that he puts Poe and his 'character' in the same position as I had *symbolized* for him in 'The Tunnel' section."[1] Williams talks of the need for the truly American poet to descend to the "ground" for the source of his poetry.

> Poe can be understood only in a knowledge of his deep roots. The quality of the flower will then be seen to be normal, in all its tortured spirituosity and paleness, a desert flower with roots under the sand of his day. Whitman had to come from under. All have to come from under and through a dead layer...(The poet) wants to have the feet of his understanding on the ground, his ground, *the* ground, the only ground that he knows, that which *is* under his feet. I speak of aesthetic satisfaction. This want, in America, can only be filled by knowledge, a poetic knowledge, of that ground.[2]

It is Poe, according to Williams, who "gives the sense for the first time in America, that literature is *serious*, not a matter of courtesy but of truth."[3] Repudiating the formless masses and their wholesale transposition of European culture to

America, he sought to develop and enforce his own method
of forming the elements in which he lived; but, his method
"failing, truth turning to love, as if metamorphosed in his
hands as he was about to grasp it," he became "defenseless,
the place itself attacked him," and he was forced to despair.[4]
Thus Poe symbolizes the American search for a truly local,
hence original, ground for "aesthetic satisfaction," and the
failure to find it through intellectual method alone. He stands
as both promise and threat to the poet who would attempt
the creation of a Bridge "synoptic of all tides below."

"The Tunnel" begins in Manhattan at night, as "lights/
Channel the congresses" of people, the "Refractions of the
thousand theatres, faces," along Broadway "Up Times Square
to Columbus Circle." The streams of people recall the famous
image from *The Waste Land* (Eliot accepted "The Tunnel"
for publication in *Criterion*), and the diffusion and refrac-
tion of light suggests that the city itself is one of those "panoramic sleights" that are "never disclosed, but hastened to
again," night after night after night, abounding in "perform-
ances, assortments, resumes," masks and masques that con-
ceal rather than reveal. These surface "refractions" of "theatres, faces" that flow towards Columbus Circle form the river
of modern, urban time, the destructive element in which the
imagination must immerse itself if it is to assimilate "by
heart" and move beyond: "...You shall search them all./
Some day by heart you'll learn each famous sight/ And watch
the curtain lift in hell's despite;/ You'll find the garden in the
third act dead,/ Finger your knees, and wish yourself in bed/
With tabloid crime-sheets perched in easy sight." The images
of the "famous sight" and the "garden in the third act"
which is "dead" suggest that the historical and traditional
are mere "archeology." The return to Eden, the "third act"
of the Christian myth, isn't even as convincing (or entertain-
ing) as the "tabloid crime-sheets" that reflect the enterprises
accompanying the Fall. The failure of these "refractions" to

satisfy the hunger for unity or the dream of act associates them with the passive "bed," a dreamland where "easy sight" is romantic and illusory.

The poet, an unindividuated "you" at this point in his descent, as usual "will meet the scuttle yawn:/ The subway yawns the quickest promise home;" and as he moves toward the subway there is repeated the symbol of the unity toward which he unknowingly advances: "Out of the Square, the Circle burning bright." On his way he is ironically cautioned: "Avoid the glass doors gyring at your right,/ Where boxed alone a second, eyes take fright/ —Quite unprepared rush naked back to light:/ And down beside the turnstile press the coin/ Into the slot. The gongs already rattle." The image of eyes "boxed alone" recalls the deflection of vision where "each sees only his dim past reversed" mentioned as a quality of the labyrinth in "Cape Hatteras"; this recognition of the reverse vision of the modern bedlam is what the bedlamite must avoid if he is to continue to believe in the sufficiency of the labyrinth. And, paradoxically, this recognition is precisely what is necessary if he is to be reborn in terms of the imagination, to emerge "naked" in the light and stay there.

In the subway the manifold refractions of the street lights give way to the monotone of motion and the monotony of the repetitious conversation "of other faces, also underground." The "overtone of motion/ underground" reduces all the conversations on board to meaningless remnants, stitches. The subway system is imagistically linked with the human brain, that source of the "theorems sharp as hail" ("Cape Hatteras") which threaten to destroy life itself: "The phonographs of hades in the brain/ Are tunnels that rewind themselves, and love/ A burnt match skating in a urinal—". Stasis, repetitious motion rather than the harmonious equilibrium which the imagination seeks in the Bridge and its "whispers antiphonal," is the product of this "hades in the brain"; and the tunnel is the artifact wrought according to this mental plan. The lack of liberty and love is imaged by the "burnt match skating in a urinal," a degradation of the Lady Liberty.

The pain and confusion of the subway call up the figure of Edgar Allan Poe, that American poet who sought to turn the powers of intellect to the services of the imagination and art: "Whose head is swinging from the swollen strap?/ Whose body smokes along the bitten rails,/ Bursts from a smoldering bundle far behind/ In back forks of the chasms of the brain,—/ Puffs from a riven stump far out behind/ In interborough fissures of the mind...?" The separation of head from body, of mind from organic vitality, characterizes Poe and his poetic methodology. His body is left behind, in terms of his art, "in back forks of the chasms of the brain," as his severed head swings from the swollen strap by which he sought to hold his balance on the iron horse of mental method. The swollen strap recalls the "empty trapeze" of the stripper's "flesh" in "National Winter Garden." The suggestion is that Poe was severed by that swing instead of lugged back "lifeward" from the necessary death in the flesh, for as Williams says, Poe couldn't accept love in place of the intellectual truth he sought. One of the forms of the "Gates of Wrath" is the gate of love in the flesh, and the "Western Path" can only be found after submission to the "kiss of our agony." As one of the broken conversations of "The Tunnel" asks: "...if/ you don't like my gate why did you/ swing on it, why *didja*/ swing on it/ anyhow—"/ And somehow anyhow swing—".

Poe, with head and body severed in "The Tunnel," symbolizes the disastrous attempt to write a poetry that ignores or represses the passion; he appears at this stage of the poet's imaginative journey as a warning and a threat, for the broken, meaningless conversation of the subway is dangerous in the extreme to the imagination's unitive desire, and the mind's degradation of love could be for the poet, as it was for Poe,

an insurmountable barrier: "And why do I often meet your
visage here,/ Your eyes like agate lanterns—on and on/ Below the toothpaste and the dandruff ads?/ —And did their
riding eyes right through your side,/ And did their eyes like
unwashed platters ride?/ And Death, aloft,—gigantically
down/ Probing through you—toward me, O evermore!"
The image of Poe's "eyes like agate lanterns"[5] flashing "on
and on" recalls the derelict sailor of "Cutty Sark" whose
"eyes pressed through green glass" and shone like neon
lights, as well as Whitman's whose "Sea eyes and tidal, undenying, bright with myth" accepted all the sufferings and
destruction of war as concomitant with the imagination's
unitive life, and was thereby able to forge a new-bound pact
of love. The key to the difference between Whitman and Poe
lies in the image of "undenying" eyes, as the poet suggests
in his final question of Poe: "And when they dragged your
retching flesh,/ Your trembling hands that night through
Baltimore—/ That last night on the ballot rounds, did you/
Shaking, did you deny the ticket, Poe?" The "ticket" refers
to the Baltimore election incident which led directly to Poe's
death. As Hervey Allen maintains in his 1926 biography of
Poe, the poet was imprisoned in a Whig "coop" for several
days, subdued by whiskey and drugs, and finally forced to
vote repeatedly for the Whig ticket. Poe's denial of the ticket,
then, would have been the final assertion of his mind over his
"retching flesh"; but Crane's rhetorical question and the allusion to Poe's death are reminders that assimilation must
precede any unitive assertion in the world of *The Bridge*.

After the poet's encounter with Poe the train prepares for
the final dive beneath the River of time itself. The subway
stops to let off those who would not go under the River, and
they ascend "above where streets/ Burst suddenly in rain,"
there failing to find a refuge from the deluge that must be
undergone if Atlantis is to be raised. The subway then proceeds to the Tunnel under the River. The recurrent gongs

(recall the "gongs in white surplices" of "The Harbor Dawn") herald the second phase of the trip, the nadir of the "curve-ship" of the Bridge (that "altar" of "Proem") in a subtle in-version of the Elevation of the Host at Mass. Not unity but disjunction is signalled by these unreligious gongs, for the subway "Lets go" and winging newspapers scatter toward "corners" of that imprisoning square that threatens the uni-tive circle. The poet sinks further beneath the River and dark-ness in an atmosphere of "galvothermic" thunder, control and will defeated, in a situation recalling Columbus amidst the tempest in "Ave Maria." At this stage he encounters the "Genoese" "Wop washerwoman," the modern metamor-phosis of the Virgin, who herself has left the heights of "gaunt sky-barracks," the office building where she scrubs, to take the subway "home." The poet's question of her re-calls his question of Whitman in "Cape Hatteras" ("tell me, Walt Whitman, if infinity/ Be still the same as when you walked the beach..."), for he is equally sceptical at this point of his journey: "And does the Daemon take you home, also,/ Wop washerwoman, with the bandaged hair?.../ O Genoese, do you bring mother eyes and hands/ Back home to children and to golden hair?" The ideal of Love figured in the Virgin, and even the childhood hope of the mother's smile, are reduced to this washerwoman riding the Daemon subway; she is subjected to the same fate as the poet himself, and obviously cannot serve as an ideal or liberating agent, "high and cool," from whom aid may be implored.

This recognition casts the poet back on the Daemon sub-way itself, the machine that in fact does take the poet "home." The subway offers as substitute for the liberating mother's smile a "demurring and eventful yawn" that threat-ens to swallow the poet whole. To return home the poet must proceed through these mechanical gates of wrath, must assimilate this new threat to the imagination's unitive life. The parody of rebirth that the subway offers ("the quickest promise home") is imaged as the frustration of spiritual, imaginative rebirth: "Whose hideous laughter is a bellows mirth/ —Or the muffled slaughter of a day in birth—/ O cruelly to inoculate the brinking dawn/ With antennae toward worlds that glow and sink;—/ To spoon us out more liquid than the dim/ Locution of the eldest star, and pack/ The conscience navelled in the plunging wind,/ Umbilical to call—and straightway die!" The "brinking dawn" is the female principle which the phallic subway impregnates ("inoculates"); but the children of this union, the modern bedlamites, are severed from their natural parentage, their "conscience navelled in the plunging wind" with the remnant of the umbilical cord to "straightway die." The fragmenting action of the Faustian Daemon is here suggested in the severing of "conscience" (not the moralist's sense of right and wrong, ethical classifications, etc.), that apprehension of "knowledge with," of the union of man and the rest of the living universe. This fragmentation of the modern "conscience" and consciousness of the human relationship with other life forms is the true threat, and no amount of material comfort can substitute for this loss of the unitive, spiritual imaginative life. The traditional moral (religious) ideals have given way to the "aesthetic satisfaction" of unity, that "conscience" which is the goal of the imagination's life. It is this type of "knowledge" toward which Columbus moved at the end of "Ave Maria," and which the poet of *The Bridge* now seeks.

In this subway bedlam beneath the River occurs the nadir of submission to the forces of the Faustian intellect, an agony imaged as a "kiss" in a paradox recalling the scrutiny of God in "Ave Maria," as he searched "Cruelly with love" his "parable of man." It is the moment of atonement, the fusion of time and eternity in the act of total surrender, death. The bits and snatches of subway conversation, "shrill ganglia/ Impassioned with some song we fail to keep," is the voice of time which sounds before the poet's resurrection

into the imagination's "Everpresence." It is the quintessence
of negative capability, in terms of the poetic creation (a relationship of course paralleled by that of the Atonement to
the Resurrection), as the poet lies waiting for the "pure impulse inbred" of the creative imagination: "And yet, like
Lazarus, to feel the slope,/ The sod and billow breaking,—
lifting ground,/ A sound of waters bending astride the sky/
Unceasing with some Word that will not die." This "Word"
is a renewal of the "inmost sob, half heard" by which Columbus calmed the tempest, of that "stilly note" that in "Quaker
Hill" transmuted silence. It is the epiphany of the only Absolute to which Crane ascribed, that of the imagination itself,
which can "start some white machine that sings" the imagination's truth. The imagination, like Lazarus, is by its own
power raised from the death in the Tunnel, feeling the life
force shared by "sod and billow" as it moves "upward from
the dead" with a new bound pact.

An asterisk separates this resurrection out of the Tunnel
from the conclusion of "The Tunnel." The poet has been liberated from the Daemon subway, and individuated as well,
for he shifts to the first person in this conclusion. He has
been lugged back "lifeward" after the death in time and the
flesh, as the initial image of the "tugboat" lunging up the
River of time suggests, and now what remains is to create his
Bridge. He has discovered the immortal power of the imagination *within himself*, the Word that endures beyond the death
of "shrill ganglia" and the kiss of agony that spends out the
passions. He stands beside the River: "I counted the echoes
assembling, one after one,/ Searching, thumbing the midnight
on the piers./ Lights, coasting, left the oily tympanum of
waters;/ The blackness somewhere gouged glass on a sky."
The poet has now fused these attentuations of shrill ganglia
into echoes of the unitive, living Word, joining the voices of
time with the Word of eternity and the Everpresent imagination. He has learned "by heart," fusing them with his own

pure impulse inbred. He searches them as he would a book, "thumbing the midnight" and its blackness that puts out the eyes of the Cyclopean towers of the city, reading the echoing reverberations of his unitive Word. The "thousand theatres, faces" that lined the way from Times Square to Columbus Circle, light refractions, here become internalized, as city lights go out and the poet listens to midnight echoes of these refractions fused with the Word that wells up within him. The tenses of this concluding section progress from past to present to future, as the poet expands the significance of his act by postulating it as eternally recurrent (as indeed it has been proved throughout *The Bridge*):

> Tossed from the coil of ticking towers....Tomorrow,
> And to be....Here by the River that is East—
> Here at the waters' edge the hands drop memory;
> Shadowless in that abyss they unaccounting lie.
> How far away the star has pooled the sea—
> Or shall the hands be drawn away, to die?
>
> Kiss of our agony Thou gatherest,
>   O Hand of Fire
>   gatherest—

The imagination has successfully passed through the Gates of Wrath, tossed from the time-measuring towers of the city towards morning ("morrow") and the future; and now it stands liberated in the present. The past is symbolically laid to rest in the River of time, as the "hands drop memory" in the abyss of the Harbor. The search without has ceased, as hands "lie unaccounting," inactive but potent. The transition from images of eyes to those of hands suggests that the stages of recognition and assimilation have been passed through, and that the poet now waits for the stage of creation, making, building. Standing on land, the poet feels the pull of the sea, beckoning him to final rest and death in its abyss.

In this moment of "power in repose" the poet invokes the "Hand of Fire," the instrument of creation that can build a Bridge *over* the sea to the stars and Love, as he prepares to realize his dream of act.

CHAPTER 11

Atlantis

"Atlantis," the concluding section of *The Bridge*, is the culmination of one long process and the beginning of another.
At the end of "The Tunnel" the imagination waited for the
advent of the "Hand of Fire," its own Promethean force of
imaginative redemption and creation that could lift night and
lend a myth to God. The poet had "counted the echoes" of
earlier attempts to move up the River of Time to its source,
and had exhausted the possibilities of such a remembrance of
history or his own past experiences. Thus he had dropped
"memory" into the abyss of the harbor and fully submitted
himself to the destructive element of the "Kiss of our
agony." The imagination's dream of act is submersed with
the poet's hands, the agents of creative action; and it can
only wait and pray for the "Hand of Fire" to come. Atlantis,
the mythical island reputed to be the origin of language and
laws in Western civilization, is the symbol for the poet of
that "attitude of spirit" which, like Columbus's Cathay, is
characterized by the apprehension of the absolute and timeless truth of the imagination. And the action of the "Atlantis" section is the successful reaching and realization of that

"attitude of spirit," that mythic state emergent from the abysmal ocean. This discovery of that mythic state provides the impetus for the imagination's act of writing *The Bridge*, the record of how the discovery, the conjugation of "infinity's dim marge," was made "Anew." Thus "Atlantis" concludes the imagination's search, via the poet, for that mythic state, and begins the process by which it performs the act of writing the poem, hurling its own "mythic spear." It is this final act that makes *The Bridge* itself a Bridge to that "attitude of spirit," a span over which society may cross by reading the poem. The imagination thus emulates the epic hero, redeeming society by its act, defining itself as savior.

The poet's movement from the harbor of Manhattan to Atlantis is effected through the agency of the symbolic Bridge. The revelation of the Bridge wrought by the "Hand of Fire" can only be described as an epiphany, and yet one that has been thoroughly prepared for. The Bridge is perceived as the "index of night," the key to the book which the poet had been "thumbing" hopelessly at the end of "The Tunnel," and its appearance is as inspirational and involuntary as that of the purifying "Hand of Fire." But the poet's preparation for its appearance, his searching (learning "by heart") progress through the earlier stages of the poem, has enabled him to perceive the full mythic significance of the epiphany. He sees the Bridge "condense eternity," press: "—Tomorrows into yesteryear—and link/ What cipher-script of time no traveller reads/ But who, through smoking pyres of love and death,/ Searches the timeless laugh of mythic spears." The learning experience necessary to the imagination's growth toward the unitive act has been both internal and external, as it has learned new terms by which to define its sensibility and has grown internally toward a recognition of its synthesizing, parabolic, relationship to the body and mind, passion and reason. Thus its discovery-recognition of the symbolic Bridge is a perception-creation: the Bridge is symbolic because it is revealed as the structure which unifies the objects and events which the imagination has encountered and assimilated in its life. The relationship between poet and Bridge is similar to that between Columbus and the "inmost sob, half-heard," and by implication half-spoken, in "Ave Maria." The unitive act, like the act of creation in Crane's poetics, is not the result of will only but of inspiration, the epiphany of the "Hand of Fire" or the harmonizing sound of the "inmost sob, half-heard," half-spoken. In "Atlantis" the poet comes to realize that the Myth of the Bridge is just such an "intrinsic Myth" of the "Everpresence" of the "pure impulse inbred," the life of the imagination in man.

This relationship of the "intrinsic Myth" of the creative imagination to the poet, and its existence beyond the control of will, is suggested in a letter Crane wrote on the subject of the creative act:

> The actual fleshing of a concept is so complex and difficult, however, as to be quite beyond the immediate avail of will or intellect. A fusion with other factors not so easily named is the condition of fulfillment. It is alright to call this "possession," if you will, only it should not be insisted that its operation denies the simultaneous function of a strong critical faculty. It is simply a stronger focus than can be arbitrarily willed into operation by the ordinarily-employed perceptions.[1]

It is this "possession" (the "white seizure" in "Atlantis") by the "intrinsic" power of the creative imagination that is the Myth of the Bridge, the myth of the act of bridging whereby the truth of the imagination, or Atlantis, is reached. This "possession" lies beyond the avail of will, as does the creation of the Bridge, a fact the poet acknowledged in "Proem": "How could mere toil align thy choring strings!" The "Hand of Fire" that makes the Brooklyn Bridge the "Bridge of Fire" is the creative imagination, and its appearance is of the nature of epiphany, a rebirth, a revelation of the poet to himself that enables him to act.

As the previous discussion has suggested, myth is central to the "Atlantis" section; and specifically, the Myth of the Bridge. The island of the title is, of course, a mythical island; and within the section there are allusions to Tyre and Troy, Jason and Aeolus. More importantly, the symbolic Bridge becomes for the poet an "intrinsic Myth" by which he crosses to a state of consciousness symbolized by Atlantis, which has more affinity with myth than, say, the rational "theorems" of "Cape Hatteras" or the reflective stoicism of "Quaker Hill." By enabling the poet to reach Atlantis the Bridge has answered the invocation of "Proem" that it "lend a myth to God," at least for the poet; for it must always be held in mind that the progression through the poem is the progression of the imagination via the objective-correlative of a fictional poet (poet because he does progress toward the writing of the poem) through states of consciousness, attitudes, and emotions toward the final "absolute" state of "Atlantis." The imagination's life is the fundamental subject of *The Bridge*: the infinity "conjugated" is the modern imagination itself, for infinity in the poem is the imagination's "Everpresence." It is this process of growth which allows *The Bridge* to be itself a Bridge for other readers, as in Crane's poetics it is the new "condition of life" embodied in the living artifact of a poem that begets in the reader "new spiritual articulations."

Thus, the poet's allusions to other myths as models for his act in "Atlantis," and his identification of the Bridge as "intrinsic Myth," suggests that in this final section of *The Bridge* he enters into a mythic mode of consciousness. By a mythic mode of consciousness I mean also a mythopoeic mode, in which the consciousness is liberated from the mediated vision of reality of the reflective mind and empowered to directly create a myth. This type of consciousness recreates both subject and object in the act of perception. It is mythic in the sense that its act is grounded in the activity of the "absolute and timeless"[2] creative imagination, and as Crane noted "is quite beyond the immediate avail of will or intellect." The mythopoeic mode of consciousness is, especially, a mode of being, as poets have so often insisted, rather than merely another way of doing—the intrinsic Myth of the Bridge, the poet finally recognizes, is "iridescently upborne/ Through the bright drench and fabric of our veins." The poet's perception of the Bridge signals a change of state (he's now able to read the message of the Bridge, the unity of the "cipher-script of time," as he was not before), and his ultimate perception of the Bridge is that he himself is a Bridge, that the "steeled Cognizance" of the Bridge bears witness to the intrinsic Myth of the imagination which he himself possesses and is possessed by. Thus his perception of the Bridge has recreated him (or signalled his recreation), as it liberates him from time into the eternity of "Atlantis." His perception has also recreated the Bridge, moving it from the literal to the symbolic. The Brooklyn Bridge has always been there, but the poet's ability to perceive it and use it symbolically has not. Thus the poet's unitive act, symbolized by the perception-creation of the Bridge, enables him to move to that state of consciousness symbolized by Atlantis.

That the poet's perception of the "harp and altar" of the Bridge leads to his recognition of love as the kind of knowledge implicit in the imagination's truth is suggested by the epigraph (from Plato's *Symposium*) to the section: "Music is then the knowledge of that which relates to love in harmony and system." The Bridge is imaged as musical instrument: a harp with "choiring strings," and a "Choir" translating the voice of time into the "Psalm of Cathay," an act which is Love's "white, pervasive Paradigm." And at the end of "Atlantis" music and instrument are conjoined in "One Song, one Bridge of Fire," which leaps toward the "Everpresence, beyond time" of Atlantis and of Love. The identification of Atlantis, symbol of the imagination's unitive truth, and Love, suggests that Love is indeed the object of the poet's journey. Further, the "pity" that "steeps the grass" at the conclusion of the poem is etymologically associated with the more overtly religious "piety," as well as that state of love which Blake termed "pity." In short, the identification of Atlantis and a state of Love in which "the cities are endowed/ And justified conclamant with ripe fields," in which time and space are harmonized and fused in one moment and state that puts "The serpent with the eagle in the leaves," is for Crane an identification of aesthetic and moral truth. The identification thus allows *The Bridge* to "lend a myth to God" in terms of the absolute of the truth of the imagination.

The justification in terms of the poem of the introduction of Love, and of the final identification of aesthetic and moral truth, of the imagination and Love, has seemed to some insufficient.[3] But from the beginning of *The Bridge*, in the submerged metaphor of the Bridge as the Madonna in "Proem," Love has been vitally linked with the unitive act of the imagination. In "Ave Maria" it is the Virgin to whom Columbus prays for cessation of the storm and safe passage back to Spain. In "Powhatan's Daughter" the Dance of Maquokeeta is performed at least partially because "Pocahontas grieves," and the unification of the cosmos in terms of the Indian myth is accomplished under the aegis of Pocahontas. Imaginatively impotent characters such as the hoboes of "The River" and the derelict sailor of "Cutty Sark" are characterized by their wifelessness, their lack of love-relationships. The poet in his childhood considers his mother's loving smile, delivered once only, as "Sabbatical" and liberating. Whitman is credited with having achieved an imaginative, poetic, rendering of the imagination's truth in terms of "living brotherhood." "Three Songs" obviously deal with love, and the final one, "Virginia," renders an attempt to "build" love out of a song to a common secretary. "Quaker Hill" associated the poetic, unitive act of imagination with a shielding of "love from despair." And "The Tunnel" introduces the "Wop washerwoman," a mother figure again, as a dubious agent of love on the subway. Obviously, various aspects of Love are figured in these differing characters, each appropriate to the section of the poem and the state of the imagination's growth in which they appear. But if the Bridge is truly "one arc synoptic of all tides below," it requires little stretch of the imagination to perceive the "Love" of "Atlantis" as symbolic of all its aspects previously rendered in the concrete. After all, the love suggested in the epigraph from Plato is a generalized love, a pervasive condition of life rendered sympathetically and symphonically in the music it begets, music which itself (as a medium) bespeaks a generalization not only from particular life-instances but from words themselves, as evidenced by the inarticulate but symphonic "whispers antiphonal" at the conclusion of "Atlantis."

Thus reaching Atlantis signals the liberation of the poet into a state of consciousness characterized by apprehension of the universality of sympathetic love as well as by the unity of the "world dimensional" and the eternal, ubiquitous truth of the imagination. It is a truly mythic mode of consciousness, for the poet is liberated into a world where the laws of his imagination have become the laws of the universe, where his "dream of act" can be transformed into reality, where action and being coincide in direct immediacy. It is in the reaching of Atlantis that the identification of the aesthetic and the moral implicit in Crane's poetic theory is achieved. The connection is suggested in many ways, as for instance the poet's recognition that the myth of the Bridge to Love has as its central event the eternal return of the original act of creation of "Deity's young name." It is always new, always original, and a continual re-achievement of that mode of consciousness symbolized by the discovery of Atlantis or Cathay, that "attitude of spirit." The "canticle" of the Bridge, the imagination's union of all things under the aegis of universal love,

is always the same. The unitive act is always the same: "rapt
inception and beatitude," the assimilation and recreation of
the present (and the poet too) in terms of the truth of the
imagination, which bespeaks the Everpresence of Love. In
this state of absolute beauty or "beatitude" the Beautiful and
the Good and True unite: "In this condition there may be
discoverable under new forms certain spiritual illuminations,
shining with a morality essentialized from experience directly, and not from previous precepts or preconceptions."[4] The
Beautiful, the embodiment of the truth of the imagination, is
also the beatific, and the achievement of this state of "absolute beauty" is made possible by the creation of a Bridge to
"God."

The movement toward this unitive goal is evident in the
tripartite structure of "Atlantis." The first section, stanzas
one through six, renders the harmonizing and pervasive lifting of night by the Bridge, the mediating force linking time
and eternity, earth and stars, in its act of harmonious and
universal Love, its "Psalm of Cathay." In this section the
poet moves from description to direct address of the Bridge,
and the "white, pervasive paradigm" of "Love" which the
Song of the choiring strings of the Bridge articulates. The
poet assumes the attitude of the undifferentiated observer in
this initial stage of recognition of the power and mythic im-
port of the Bridge. He is not passive, for his "eyes, like sea-
gulls stung with rime," pick their way up the "towering
looms" of the Bridge. But he is unindividuated at this point
from travellers in general, and hence liable, like Jason (whom
he addresses), to shipwreck and loss of the word of his new
discovery. It is not enough to see the golden fleece or Cathay
—a record of that discovery must be brought "home."

In the second section of "Atlantis," stanzas seven through
ten, the imagination generalizes the fictional "I" and separates his person from the Bridge: "We left the haven hanging
in the night." From this new vantage point he is able to see

the unitive nature of the truth that the circle of the Bridge encloses, much as the eyes of Columbus in "Ave Maria" could "accrete-enclose/ This turning rondure whole" after his uttered-answered prayer had made a bridge of the ocean. Looking "backward" now the poet can still see "the circular, indubitable frieze/ Of heaven's meditation," the Bridge and its "one song." And he turns to a reflection on the "steeled Cognizance," a poetic meditation possessing a solemnal tone and rhythm that recalls Columbus's own Te Deum to the "incognizable Word/ of Eden and the enchained Sepulchre." The Bridge at this point is a living artifact symbolic of "heaven's meditation" embodying its own mythic truth completely. The poet knows this truth, having participated in it in the first section of "Atlantis," just as Columbus, having come through the stormy seas, knew the "truth" of the incognizable Word that saved him. In other words, the poet at this point has assimilated the "truth" of the Bridge; and to bear witness to his new knowledge he addresses the Bridge as "Swift peal of secular light, intrinsic Myth...iridescently upborne/ Through the bright drench and fabric of our veins." Having picked "biting way" up the Bridge, and then separated himself from it, he can now recognize the internalization of the "truth" of the Bridge within himself—he had put on its knowledge with its mythic power, which is now "leading" him from "time's realm" to the "Everpresence, beyond time" of the state of universal Love of which the Bridge's song is "Paradigm." Significantly, the poem shifts to "Forever" and "Always" to describe the eternal presence of the "white seizure" of the poet by the intrinsic Myth of the creative imagination and its "Kinetic" truth.

The third and concluding section of "Atlantis," the final two stanzas, completes the ascending individuation of the poet, as he becomes the "floating singer" of the myth of the Bridge. The poet asks "Thy pardon for this history, whitest flower," as he has at last reached Atlantis (and the Love imaged as flower in "ATLANTIS ROSE" of "Cutty Sark"). He has been delivered up from the ocean of time by the power of love liberated within him by his assimilation-perception of the "steeled Cognizance" of the Bridge. He has been recreated and liberated from time by the unitive act symbolized by the Bridge. He is a bedlamite reborn into the "Everpresence" of the imagination and the Love that drives it, into the mythic state of Atlantis. Time and space, love and hope, fuse in the primal images of the final lines, as the poet asks: "......Is it Cathay,/ Now pity steeps the grass and rainbows ring/ The serpent with the eagle in the leaves...?" Now that unity and harmony have been established by the perception-creation of "One Song, one Bridge of Fire," is it Cathay? Has the discovery been made of that "attitude of spirit" which bespeaks the truth of the imagination, which Crane called the "genetic basis of all speech, hence consciousness and thought-extension"[5] that provides the impetus for "new spiritual articulations" and fulfillment of the Sanskrit charge?

The answer to this question is affirmative, and affirmative of the entire life of *The Bridge*: "Whispers antiphonal in azure swing." This concluding line of the poem, itself antiphonal of the "multitudinous Verb" displayed in the movement from "Ave Maria" to "Atlantis," possesses a surety of tone and rhythm which bespeaks that "power in repose" that Hart Crane knew to be "the source and antecedent of all motion." The dymanic stasis of "Whispers antiphonal" recalls in theme and measured movement the Proem's image of the Bridge, "Implicitly thy freedom staying thee!" But here at the end of the poem exclamation is not necessary, for the poet no longer speaks to the Bridge but through it, in unison, with "One Song, one Bridge of Fire." The music of the human voice, muted into whisperings, beginnings of speech, swings free in the azure dawn, as the poet begins to wake from the "dream" of act into action itself. He will fulfill his Sanskrit charge by rendering in words, poetry, his discovery of Cathay, in order that Cathay might be brought back to his people. The final word of the line, the verb "swing," recalls the prayer for a "curveship" to "lend a myth to God," and emphasizes the recurrent nature of the act of curveship (worship). Implicit in dynamic stasis, motion in repose, is open form and further motion, "still one shore beyond desire," as the entire poem has attested to the truth of the fact that new conditions of life germinate new spiritual articulations. The imagination has defined its act as a Bridge "translating time" into speech, recording the "multitudinous Verb" of its life in the poem itself, and the "whispers antiphonal" which conclude *The Bridge* also signal a beginning, the beginning of the fulfillment of its "dream of act" in the utterance of the poem. The movement to light has been concluded, and the imagination is at one and at peace with the universe, a harmonious state achieved not through stoic resignation but through active acceptance and assimilation of the vitality and energy evinced by all creation. The poem ends in affirmation of the organic process to which it owes its life, a process of human poetic creation that affirms the whole of the living world.

NOTES

Chapter 1

1 Hart Crane, "General Aims and Theories," in Philip Horton, *Hart Crane: The Life of an American Poet* (New York, 1957), pp. 326-27.

2 Allen Tate, *Reactionary Essays* (New York, 1936); and Yvor Winters, "The Progress of Hart Crane," *Poetry* XXVI (June, 1930), pp. 153-65.

3 Allen Tate, "A Poet and His Life," *Poetry* L (July, 1937), p. 223.

4 Allen Tate, "Hart Crane," in *The Man of Letters in the Modern World* (New York, 1955), p. 290.

5 R.P. Blackmur, *The Double Agent* (New York, 1935), p. 121.

6 *The Letters of Hart Crane*, ed. Brom Weber (Berkeley and Los Angeles, 1965), number 343; p. 353. Hereafter cited as *Letters*; my citations are to the letter numbers, and to the page numbers.

7 L.S. Dembo, *Hart Crane's Sanskrit Charge: A Study of "The Bridge"* (Ithaca, New York, 1960), p. 10.

8 Dembo, p. 31.

9 R.W.B. Lewis, *The Poetry of Hart Crane: A Critical Study* (Princeton, 1967), p. 382.

10 Dembo, p. 16.

11 Lewis, p. 380.

12 *Letters*, 289, p. 308.

13 *Letters*, 289, p. 308.

14 *Letters*, 234, p. 239.

15 Wallace Stevens, *The Necessary Angel* (New York, 1951), p. 25.

16 Hart Crane, "General Aims and Theories," in Philip Horton, *Hart Crane: The Life of an American Poet* (New York, 1957), p. 328.

17 *Letters*, 239, pp. 244-45.

18 *Letters*, 137, p. 128.

19 "General Aims and Theories," p. 327.

20 Stevens, p. 29.

21 *Letters*, 142, p. 132.

22 "General Aims and Theories," p. 324.

Chapter 2

1 ["Letter to H. Monroe,"] in Horton, p. 332.

2 *Letters*, 289, p. 305.

3 *Letters*, 289, p. 305.

4 *Letters*, 289, p. 305.

5 "General Aims and Theories," pp. 324-25.

6 *Letters*, 234, p. 238. Crane affirmed his belief that the act of creation itself was the true subject of art in a comment on the basis of "truth" in Plato. 'What you admire in Plato as "divine sanity" is the architecture of his logic. Plato doesn't live today because of the intrinsic "truth" of his statements: their only living truth today consists in the fact of their harmonious relationship to each other in the context of his organization of them. This grace partakes of poetry....No wonder Plato considered the banishment of poets;—their reorganization of chaos on basis perhaps divergent from his own threatened the logic of his system, itself founded on assumptions that demanded the very defense of poetic construction which he was fortunately able to provide."

7 See Sr. M. Bernetta Quinn, *The Metamorphic Tradition in Modern Poetry* (New Brunswick, 1955), for an interesting discussion of metamorphosis in *The Bridge*.

8 *Letters*, 261, p. 274.

9 *Letters*, 254, p. 268.

10 "General Aims and Theories," p. 324.

11 "General Aims and Theories," p. 324.

12 Soren Kierkegaard, *Philosophical Fragments*, trans David F. Swenson (New York, 1936), p. 29.

13 "General Aims and Theories," p. 327.

14 "General Aims and Theories," p. 327.

15 "Letter to H. Monroe," pp. 330 and 332.

16 "General Aims and Theories," p. 328.

17 "General Aims and Theories," p. 326.

18 "General Aims and Theories," p. 328.

19 "General Aims and Theories," p. 326.

20 "Letter to H. Monroe," p. 333.

21 "General Aims and Theories," p. 328.

22 Susan Sontag, *Against Interpretation and Other Essays*, p. 21.

Chapter 3

1 Rollo May, *Psychology and the Human Dilemma* (Princeton, 1967), p. 103.

Chapter 4

1 *Letters*, 254, p. 268.

2 *Letters*, 289, p. 306.

Chapter 5

1 *Letters*, 289, p. 306.

2 *Letters*, 289, p. 306.

3 *Letters*, 289, p. 306.

4 *Letters*, 289, p. 306.

5 Stevens, p. 61.

6 *Letters*, 289, p. 306.

7 *Letters, 289, pp. 306-307.*

8 *Letters*, 289, p. 307.
9 *Letters*, 289, p. 307.
10 *Letters*, 289, p. 307.
11 *Letters*, 289, p. 307.
12 The religious imagery here is obvious enough, and the alternating ironical lines, as well as the mention of the "charter" and the "promised crown," recall the poetry of Emily Dickinson. Similarly, the mention of "Eldorado" recalls Poe's famous poem. Both poets are later invoked in *The Bridge* as followers of the imagination's "God."

Chapter 8

1 *Letters*, 259, p. 272.
2 *Letters*, 289, p. 305.

Chapter 10

1 *Letters*, 265, p. 278.
2 William Carlos Williams, *In the American Grain* (New York, 1956), p. 213.
3 Williams, *In the American Grain*, p. 216.
4 Williams, *In the American Grain*, p. 232.
5 The image of Poe's eyes "like agate lanterns" echoes Poe's own image of the beautiful Helen standing with "agate lamp" in hand ("To Helen"). The borrowing is ironic, for here Poe inhabits Hades, rather than the "Holy Land" of Helen and beauty.

Chapter 11

1 *Letters*, 239, pp. 244-245.
2 Crane, "Modern Poetry," p. 182.
3 See Hyatt Howe Waggoner, *The Heel of Elohim* (Norman, 1950).
4 "General Aims and Theories," p. 327.
5 "General Aims and Theories," p. 327.

SELECTED BIBLIOGRAPHY

Alvarez, A. *Stewards of Excellence*. New York, 1958.

Andreach, Robert J. *Studies in Structure*. New York, 1964.

Arpad, Joseph J. "Hart Crane's Platonic Myth: The Brooklyn Bridge,"
    American Literature (March, 1967), 75-86.

Bergson, Henri. *Time and Free Will*, trans. F.L. Pogson. New York,
    1960.

Blackmur, R.P. *The Double Agent*. New York, 1935.

Brooks, Cleanth. *The Hidden God*. New Haven, 1963.

Butterfield, R.W. *The Broken Arc: A Study of Hart Crane*. Edinburgh,
    1969.

Cambon, Glauco. *The Inclusive Flame*. Bloomington, 1963.

Cargill, Oscar. *Intellectual America: Ideas on the March*. New York,
    1941.

Coffman, Stanely K., Jr. "Symbolism in The Bridge," *PMLA*, LXV
    (March, 1951), 65-77.

Cowley, Malcolm. "A Preface to Hart Crane," *The New Republic*,
    62 (April 23, 1930), 276-277.

——. *Exile's Return*. New York, 1956.

Crane, Hart. *The Complete Poems and Selected Letters and Prose of
    Hart Crane*, ed. Brom Weber. New York, 1966.

——. *The Letters of Hart Crane*, ed. Brom Weber. Berkeley and Los Angeles, 1965.

Dembo, L.S. *Hart Crane's Sanskrit Charge: A Study of The Bridge*. Ithaca, 1960.

Focillon, Henri. *The Life of Forms in Art*, trans. C.B. Hogan and G. Kubler. New York, 1948.

Fowlie, Wallace. *The Clown's Grail: A Study of Love in its Literary Expression*. London, 1947.

Friedman, Paul. "*The Bridge*: A Study in Symbolism," *Psychoanalytical Quarterly*, 21 (1952), 49-80.

Hazo, Samuel. *Hart Crane: An Introduction and Interpretation*. New York, 1963.

Herman, Barbara. "The Language of Hart Crane," *The Sewanee Review*, LVIII (Winter, 1950), 52-67.

Hoffman, Frederick J. *The Twenties*. New York, 1955.

Horton, Philip. *Hart Crane: The Life of an American Poet*. New York, 1937.

Kloucek, Jerome W. "The Framework of Hart Crane's *The Bridge*," *Midwest Review* (Spring, 1960), 13-23.

Leibowitz, Herbert A. *Hart Crane: An Introduction to the Poetry*. New York, 1968.

Lewis, R.W.B. *The Poetry of Hart Crane*. Princeton, 1967.

Loveman, Samuel. *Hart Crane: A Conversation with Samuel Loveman*. New York, 1964.

Matthiessen, F.O. "An Absolute Music," *The Yale Review*, 27 (Fall, 1937), 173-175.

May, Rollo, *Psychology and the Human Dilemma*. Princeton, 1967.

Miller, James E., Jr., Shapiro, Karl, and Slote, Bernice. *Start With the Sun*. Lincoln, 1960.

Paul, Sherman. *Hart's Bridge*. Urbana, Chicago and London, 1972.

Perry, Robert L. *The Shared Vision of Waldo Frank and Hart Crane*. University of Nebraska Studies, XXXIII. Lincoln, 1966.

Poe, Edgar Allan. *The Works of Edgar Allan Poe*. New York, 1894.

Poulet, Georges. *Studies in Human Time*, trans. Elliott Coleman. Baltimore, 1956.

Quinn, Sister M. Bernetta. *The Metamorphic Tradition in Modern Poetry*. New Brunswick, 1955.

Quinn, Vincent. *Hart Crane*. New York, 1963.

Riddel, Joseph. "Hart Crane's Poetics of Failure," *ELH* (December, 1966), 473-96.

Schwartz, Joseph. *Hart Crane: An Annotated Critical Bibliography.* New York, 1970.

Shapiro, Karl. *In Defense of Ignorance.* New York, 1960.

Slote, Bernice. "Transmutation in Crane's Imagery in *The Bridge*," *MLN*, LXXIII (January, 1958), 15-23.

——. "The Structure of Hart Crane's *The Bridge*," UKCR, XXIV (March, 1958), 225-238.

Spears, Monroe K. *Hart Crane.* Minneapolis, 1965.

Swallow, Allan. *An Editor's Essays of Two Decades.* Seattle and Denver, 1962,

Tate, Allen. "A Distinguished Poet," *The Hound and Horn*, 3 (July-Summer, 1930), 580-585.

——. *Reactionary Essays.* New York, 1936.

Taylor, Frajan. "Keats and Crane: An Airy Citadel," *Accent*, VII (Autumn, 1947), 34-40.

Trachtenberg, Allan. *Brooklyn Bridge, Fact and Symbol.* New York, 1965.

Unterecker, John. "The Architecture of *The Bridge*," *Wisconsin Studies in Contemporary Literarure*, III (Spring-Summer, 1962), 5-20.

——. *Voyager: A Life of Hart Crane.* New York, 1969.

Waggoner, Hyatt Howe. *The Heel of Elohim.* Norman, 1950.

Weber, Brom. *Hart Crane: A Biographical and Critical Study.* New York, 1948.

Whitman, Walt. *The Collected Writings of Walt Whitman*, ed. Gay Wilson Allen and E. Sculley Bradley. New York, 1961.

Wilder, Amos. *The Spiritual Aspects of the New Poetry.* New York, 1940.

Williams, William Carlos. "Hart Crane (1899-1932)," *Contempo*, II (July 5, 1932), 1.

——. *In the American Grain.* New York, 1956.

Willingham, John R. "'Three Songs' of Hart Crane's *The Bridge*: A Reconsideration," *American Literature*, XXVII (March, 1955), 62-68.

Winters, Yvor. "The Progress of Hart Crane," *Poetry: A Magazine of Verse* XXXVI (June, 1930), 153-165.

——. *In Defense of Reason.* New York, 1947.

INDEX